T4-BAF-911

The Commonweal

TREASURY

GEORGE H. DUNNE
JEAN C. DE MENASCE
GEORGES BERNANOS
JOHN COGLEY
JACQUES MARITAIN
JAMES N. VAUGHAN
C. G. PAULDING
NICHOLAS A. BERDYAEV
VICTOR WHITE
KARL STERN
H. A. REINHOLD
DAVID ROSS KING
MICHAEL WILLIAMS
THOMAS MERTON
GEORGE N. SHUSTER

A SELECTION FROM THIRTY YEARS
OF THE BEST WRITING IN
THE COMMONWEAL
EDITED BY EDWARD S. SKILLIN

rice: One Dollar

The Commonweal Treasury

Edited by
EDWARD S. SKILLIN

Outstanding excerpts from The Commonweal, a review of public affairs, literature and the arts.

THE COMMONWEAL PUBLISHING CO., INC.
New York 16, N. Y.

THE COMMONWEAL TREASURY

is made up of selections from

THE COMMONWEAL READER

Printed in the United States of America

ACKNOWLEDGMENT

We wish to express our appreciation to Harper & Brothers for their kind permission to use in this book the material copyrighted by them in *The Commonweal Reader.*

The Commonweal Publishing Co., Inc.
386 Fourth Avenue
New York 16, New York

CONTENTS

What Is The Commonweal?

THE SELECTIONS which make up this book have all been taken from the pages of *The Commonweal*. In book form, as in article form, they are sure to raise questions in the minds of readers. Despite the fact that *The Commonweal* has been published every week for more than thirty years, a certain number of standard inquiries regularly arrive in the morning mail, particularly when the magazine discusses controversial issues. For instance, "Is *The Commonweal* a Catholic magazine?" — put as a challenge — is almost sure to show up after the magazine has taken a position on some highly debated public matter currently in the news, evidently because there is a popular misconception in the United States that on such matters Catholic opinion is practically unanimous.

The national debate over Senator McCarthy provides a good example. Many people found it a matter of wonder that *The Commonweal* took such a strong stand on the McCarthy question. For a certain number of Catholics, wholehearted admirers of the Senator, our opposition was embarrassing and somewhat infuriating. In some cases they were inclined to question not only *The Commonweal's* political wisdom but its editors' religious orthodoxy. An anti-McCarthy Catholic to such people was a clear contradiction in terms. The Church is anti-Communist; Senator McCarthy is anti-Communist; therefore anyone who is anti-McCarthy is pro-Communist and anti-Catholic: this dubious syllogism seemed to form the basis of their thinking on the question.

Other readers were delighted to find that *The Commonweal* echoed their own feeling about the McCarthy "crusade" and, in their efforts to counteract the widespread sympathy for Senator McCarthy in American Catholic circles, tended to exaggerate the significance of *The Commonweal* as a Catholic publication. It seems, in the light of all this, important to state just what standing *The Commonweal* does have as a Catholic publication.

During the thirty years of its life, *The Commonweal* has been generally accepted as a Catholic publication, although there is nothing in the masthead to indicate that the magazine is an organ of the Church or any official body of the Church. As a wholly independent lay weekly which is primarily concerned with the temporal order — the specific province of the layman — *The Commonweal* clearly cannot claim to speak for the Church. Its editors have not been commissioned by the Church; they certainly cannot speak with the spiritual authority of the Church, nor indeed even with the Church's temporal experience. As editors, we have often gone out of our way to make this clear in the pages of the magazine. If Senator McCarthy read *The Commonweal* with any regularity he would not have charged us, as he once did, with "falsely and dishonestly masquerading under the title of being a mouthpiece for the Catholic Church."

The Commonweal is a magazine put out by a small group of journalists who are Catholics. The magazine is no more officially Catholic than that. Its editors have no more standing in the Church than any other layman. Any authority we might have derives not from ecclesiastical status but from whatever merits we have as journalists who are specifically concerned with the meeting of the spiritual and temporal realms.

The fact, however, that we *are* Catholics and tend to see the temporal order as being directly related to the spiritual — as in the first selection in this book, Father George Dunne's "The Sin of Segregation" — surely distinguishes this magazine from similar journals of opinion. The fact that most readers of *The Commonweal* are Catholics who take a lively interest in the Church and seriously try to conform their thinking on temporal questions to their spiritual commitments also means something. Finally, most of the magazine's contributors are Catholics — some of them quite eminent Catholics and personally invested with authority which *The Commonweal* as such does not have. They write in these pages because they know that here they can quite consciously speak as Catholics. This also is not without meaning.

It is true that *The Commonweal* has a comparatively large number of non-Catholic readers. Such readers turn to the magazine because they are interested, for one reason or another, in the magazine's point of view. These readers, too, know that in *The Commonweal* they find *a* Catholic outlook on questions of the day. The same is true of *The Commonweal's* many excellent non-Catholic contributors. We conceive of the Catholic spirit as one which welcomes good thinking, good writing and good reporting wherever they are to be found. We do not believe that all wisdom — on every conceivable subject — is confined to the Catholic body or that Catholics should deprive themselves of the knowledge, insights, human understandings and plain good sense that are found outside the Church. For that reason we have always welcomed the generous support given by the many outstanding non-Catholic writers and journalists who have written for this magazine through the years. *The Commonweal* has been operated according to the principle that things are not good or true or beautiful because they are Catholic but are Catholic because they are good or true or beautiful. In the area of life where, by the very nature of things, there cannot be merely one Catholic position — where practical political and social prudence is the highest criterion — we have not hesitated to endorse what we have regarded as the better part, whether we found it within the Church or outside.

As long as *The Commonweal* continues to concern itself mainly with the thorny social and political problems of the day — dealing in concrete realities and not only in abstract principles — a large number of Catholics will continue to take strong issue with the magazine. This is as it should be. Anyone publishing a journal of opinion, Catholic or not, must count on the fact that the world is full of people with opinions of their own.

All in all, it seems to us that our critics do have a point when they challenge whether *The Commonweal* actually is a "Catholic" magazine, but the designation is not without meaning. Clearly, we are not publishing a religious magazine in the usual sense; certainly we have no ecclesiastical status. Still, there is something "Catholic" about *The Commonweal* which distinguishes it from other private journalistic ventures and it seems natural enough that it is generally thought of as a "Catholic" publication. Whether or not the magazine has a full claim to the title—which, in any case, it does not use—its readers think of *The Commonweal* as "Catholic."

Often the difficulty is gotten around by distinguishing between the "official" and the "unofficial" Catholic press. The "official" press would include the diocesan papers and by extension the clerical-edited journals as well as those put out by religious orders. The "official" nature of these papers, though, is somewhat ambiguous, too. Certainly the diocesan publication is "official" to the extent that it is used by the Bishop to communicate with his people. But in the areas where the Church does not take an "official" position — again the McCarthy issue is fresh enough to serve as a convenient example — can any editor, "official" or not, commit the Church to his personal opinion? It would seem that there was nothing more "official" in one Catholic editor's heaping praise on McCarthy than there was in *The Commonweal's* warnings of the dangers of McCarthyism. Both represent *a* Catholic opinion about Senator McCarthy's influence; neither represents *the* Catholic opinion — for the simple reason that there is no such thing.

In any discussion of *The Commonweal* it is important to underscore the fact that it is published and edited by laymen. We are fortunate enough to have among our contributors a number of outstanding clerical writers and critics. These bishops, priests and Religious are among the best writers we have. Included among the selections in this book, for example, are six by priests: "The Trappists Go to Utah" by Thomas Merton (Father Louis, O.C.S.O.); "Death and Life" by Monsignor Jean C. de Menasce; "The Hallowing of All Life" by Father H. A. Reinhold; "The Analyst and the Confessor" by Father Victor White, O.P.; "The Sin of Segregation" by Father George H. Dunne, S.J.; and "Art and Matter" by Father David Ross King. But it should be remembered that the direction, policy and general responsibility for the magazine are entirely in the hands of its lay staff. (For the benefit of our non-Catholic readers we might add that we have never been interfered with in any way by ecclesiastical superiors. We have, of course, been roundly criticized from time to time by individual priests who could not see eye to eye with us — which, given the controversial nature of the magazine, is understandable enough — but we have always been left entirely free by the proper Church authorities to size up situations as we saw them and to turn our editorial guns even on Catholic targets when, wrongly or rightly, we felt it was the thing to do.)

As a lay publication, *The Commonweal* does not pretend to be the "voice of the Catholic laity" or any such thing as that. In the first place, the Catholic laity has not appointed any group to be its voice. Secondly, there simply is no one voice of the Catholic laity. James N. Vaughan, author of "On Modern Intolerance," is a Catholic layman. In his article he obviously does not even pretend to speak for all; if he could, there would be no need for the article. The late Rabbi Wise used to say that the only thing two Jews could agree upon was what a third Jew should give to charity. All Catholics, by definition, agree on the fundamentals of their religion and on those questions which come under the heading of faith and morals. But on other matters Catholic opinions vary as much as Jewish opinions — as regular readers of the magazine know well.

The fact that *The Commonweal* reflects the views of some Catholic laymen should not be overextended. Nevertheless the magazine, as a "Catholic" periodical, does have a certain character which derives from the fact that it is lay-edited. As is fitting for a lay publication, our primary interest is in the "world," the temporal order. We do not conceive of our roles in priestly or near-priestly terms. We do not think it is our special vocation to lay down the moral law for others or to indulge in overt preaching, for instance. This is not to say that we think social, political and artistic matters can be divorced from morality or that it is proper for a group of Catholic editors to put out a magazine which does not give expression to the Christian spirit. But, in terms of the Christian vocation, it is our feeling that *The Commonweal* should serve more as a "witness" than as an apostle.

If there is one thing which distinguishes Catholicism from other religions it is that the Catholic ideal is catholic. There is in Catholicism no denial of value, however "secular" its uses. All truth — even the least "religious" in the usual sense — comes from God. Values are cherished not only because they form part of the brilliant mosaic which the Catholic view of the universe shapes into unity: they are respected for themselves, too.

Father David Ross King's "Art and Matter" is an outstanding example of this facet of Catholicism in so far as it bears on art. *The Commonweal* has long felt that it is an innocent betrayal of the Catholic spirit to despise literary or artistic values, for instance, or to subordinate them — in effect to destroy them — in order to serve some sectarian end, or an end which might be called "religious" in the institutional sense. For that reason the magazine tends to put stress on the artistic merits of books, plays and movies. In general, we believe, moral classification belongs to the province of the professional moralist. Obviously, one cannot deal with creative efforts in a moral vacuum. There are, however questions of emphasis. In the "official" Catholic press, stress is properly placed upon the moral aspects. The particular forte of this branch of the press — really an extension of the pulpit — is moral judgment. Because readers turn to the papers of their dioceses for moral judgment, as they should, the emphasis is placed on moral evaluation. A magazine like *The Commonweal* cannot presume to take over the priestly function. In this magazine the moral considerations are dealt with in the *total* consideration of the work.

As a lay publication, *The Commonweal* cannot speak for the Church or for the Catholic laity. By the same token, the magazine is comparatively free to express its own views without danger of committing the Catholic Church, even in the popular mind. No one, of course, can engage the Church where the Church refuses to be engaged. But in the case of the "official" Catholic press, there is always the danger that the errors, stupidities and prejudices, as well as the wisdom, of individual editors will be attributed to the Church itself. For that reason the responsible editor of such a publication is slow to commit his paper to any purely temporal or partisan political cause, regardless of what opinion he personally may hold. *The Commonweal* has no such restrictions. The magazine can approve or disapprove, praise or denounce as it sees fit without involving the Church or the Catholics of America. When, for instance, we endorsed Adlai Stevenson in the 1952 campaign, we committed no one but ourselves. Our endorsement was worth only whatever prestige the word of *The Commonweal* could bring it by virtue of the magazine's reputation and journalistic record after three decades of publication.

We have been asked from time to time to spell out *The Commonweal's* political philosophy. It is not an easy thing to do, because the magazine does not commit itself to any ism, party-line or partisan loyalty. In 1952 *The Commonweal* endorsed the Democratic candidate. In future campaigns, the magazine might endorse the Republican candidate, the Democratic candidate or no candidate at all. If it can be said that *The Commonweal* operates according to any political dogma, it is the right to take a fresh look at things periodically, to make all judgments tentative and to consider the total political situation, expecting the inevitable moral ambiguities, and then make a pragmatic judgment which does no violence to basic moral principles, though often enough the judgment itself — as long as politics remains in the hands of men and not angels — will be not ideal but merely the lesser of two evils. Someone has said that politics consists in making a constant series of lesser-evil choices. Certainly we have ample and depressing evidence right in the Catholic press that if one waits for the "ideal" and demands simon-pure conditions before taking any political step, he will be paralyzed into inaction, or, as happens even more frequently, he will join the angry Utopians, the perennial critics who in their own fashion fiddle sadly while Rome burns.

As Catholics, the editors of *The Commonweal* look for guidance to the social and political principles which are to be found in the papal encyclicals. The present Pope has laid down a body of wise principles which are meant to guide the individual Catholic in his thinking about the problem of war and peace. The problem of finding peace, of course, is very much the concern of the Church. In general, the Pope's directives are "internationalist," constructive and eminently practical. He has urged world cooperation, united action against aggression, the sharing of wealth and technical know-how between the have and have-not nations, and unity between all persons of good will against the materialistic dangers that threaten the civilized world. Obviously, these are general principles and not specific directions. How to apply these principles with wisdom and political prudence is a subject upon which Catholics will properly disagree. But it has been our contention that the principles are not meant to be wrapped up in pretty words and then put aside. Some applications are obvious.

It is hard, for instance, to see how so many Catholics can consistently oppose the UN and every possible manifestation of the international spirit and still pay lip-service to the recent papal directives. We do not wait on a sinless world or a wholly reformed world before setting about the business of reforming it. We do not see how we can do that and still accept the name "Catholic" as a designation for *The Commonweal,* even in the limited sense that *The Commonweal* is a "Catholic" magazine. The area of proper disagreement between Catholics is wide indeed, but we feel that the Catholic publicist simply cannot leave the papal peace program in a pious rhetorical vacuum. As George N. Shuster wisely remarks in "The Barren Tree," the concluding selection in this book, "The world will not be converted by the shudder which now runs up and down its spine."

The Commonweal's general approach, as contrasted with that of certain other Catholic journals, has been described as "liberal" — that woolliest of all woolly words. As a "liberal" magazine, *The Commonweal* quite naturally arouses the opposition of Catholics with an "un-liberal" (or "illiberal") outlook. But it should be remembered that these Catholics too have a point of view — an outlook which arouses the opposition of the Catholics who share *The Commonweal's* general approach as much as ours bothers them. If *The Commonweal* were to adopt their point of view, its violent critics then would be its present defenders. As long as the nation is loosely divided between people of a "liberal" temper and those of a "conservative" temper, it seems perfectly natural that Catholics too should be so divided. If there were no *Commonweal* to give expression to the "liberal" element among American Catholics a "liberal" magazine would have to be founded. It has been predicted — and not without reason — that if the present *Commonweal* were to fail today, almost as a sure thing a similar magazine would be on the planning boards in the morning.

Periodically in the Catholic press there is a little flurry of controversy about the "liberal Catholic." The phrase, alas, is an unfortunate one that has caused no end of misunderstanding. It suggests that, on the one hand, there is the plain old-fashioned Catholic — as one writer modestly described himself — and on the other a dubious member of the Church whose theology is shaky, whose loyalties are questionable and whose ecclesiastical standing is scandalously uncertain. This, at best, is a distorted view of the healthy division between Catholics.

The recurrent "liberal Catholic" argument is usually carried on in a fog of semantics. Many decades ago a full-blown political philosophy called Liberalism was solemnly condemned by Pope Pius IX. These days some Catholics brand the arguments of their co-religionist opponents as "liberal" and then triumphantly, if quite irrelevantly, produce this paper condemnation of Liberalism in an attempt to silence those who disagree with them. Such exercises seem pointless to us. *The Commonweal* does not describe itself as "liberal," but the designation does not upset us. Certain social and political values in American life — concern for the underdog, interracial justice and the placing of human rights before property rights, for instance — have long been described as "liberal." We endorse these values under any name. The magazine's attitude in such matters is represented in this volume by such articles as John Cogley's "L'Americano," Georges Bernanos' "Patience of the Poor" and Jacques Maritain's "That Suffer Persecution." Nowadays the "liberal" emphasis is on civil rights and the protection of our traditional democratic processes. *The Commonweal* has long fought for these values, too. It is a matter of indifference to us whether the fight is called "liberalism," called "conservatism" (which in this case may be more accurate) or called something else. The values remain worth fighting for, whatever they are called.

Happily, the word "liberal" is still sometimes used in the old-fashioned sense, not so much to describe the concrete positions one takes as to designate one's spirit and method of approach. The use of reason in controversy rather than belligerence, the absence of the chip-on-the-shoulder, the unwillingness to use the truth as if it were one's private possession, the rejection of the sectarian spirit, and the willingness to deal with others not as if the truth they have were a different kind from ours or their errors were inevitably born of malevolence — this general approach is often described, in a catch-all word, as "liberal." This approach actually represents *The Commonweal's* ideal. Unhappily, the editors and writers for this magazine do not always reach that ideal; but when we do not, we betray our own standards and, we think, the standards set for any Catholic journalist.

Father Gerald Vann, writing in *The Commonweal* a few years ago, summed up the ideal of the Catholic journalist which we have taken for our own: "It is not enough to have the truth oneself," Father Vann wrote, "in the sense of knowing the Church's teaching about the Trinity, the Incarnation and so on; truth is a question also of *mode,* of the mode of approach to other facts, other beliefs, other problems; it implies clarity but it also implies sympathy; it implies critical judgment but it also implies charity, for God Who is truth is also love. The French speak of the *vulgarisation* of theology: and the word means popularizing, it does not mean vulgarizing. Good writing is part of truth. If you take a true proposition and state it in a sentimental way, in a sectarian way, in a vulgar way, you damage the truth of it. You damage the truth itself because you distort it; you also sin against the truth inasmuch as you tend to distort or degrade the minds of your readers."

The selections from three decades of *The Commonweal* which follow cover many subjects, from politics and social problems to art and psychiatry. Each was written by a different person. They reflect both European and American thought and greatly varying personal temperaments. Yet each in its own way, we think, manifests those qualities Father Vann wrote about; each in its own way provides an answer to the question of what *The Commonweal* is and tries to be.

THE EDITORS.

The Sin of Segregation

GEORGE H. DUNNE

REV. GEORGE H. DUNNE, S.J., *who has served on the faculties of Saint Louis University and of Loyola University, Los Angeles, is well known for his writings in the field of race and labor.*

THE racist mind has contrived an almost limitless number of evasive analogies to justify the unjustifiable. They are evasive because they all ignore the crucial point which makes *racial* segregation essentially different from other kinds of segregation. It is said that if racial segregation were a violation of justice it would follow that I must admit into the circle of my intimate friends anyone who demands admittance and that I must keep perpetual open house to the whole world. The ancient sophists were more subtle than this.

We choose our friends for a variety of reasons, some good some bad, and according to a variety of tests, some consciously apprehended some known only to the subconscious. We may offend against charity by excluding certain individuals, but no one pretends that every individual has a fundamental right in justice to be accepted as an intimate friend of everyone else. You may not like my looks, you may not like my personality, you may not like my ideas. I may resent this, but I shall not charge you with injustice. I shall probably say: "Everyone to his tastes; and in any case, the feeling is mutual." But if you like everything about me except the fact that my ancestors were Irish and *for this reason alone* shut the door in my face, I shall charge you with injustice. In such an event, however, I shall not desire your friendship, because your attitude reveals a shallowness of mind that is distasteful to me. Only the snob is anxious for the friendship of snobs.

When we look honestly at this question we see that it is the advocate, not the antagonist, of racial segregation who impugns our right to choose our friends. The pattern of *racial* segregation and the prejudices which are a part of it say to me who am white: "We deny your right to include among your friends or to open your home to anyone who is of Negro ancestry. If you violate this taboo we shall cast you out of society." The social ostracism imposed upon me by a racist society is clearly an effort to interfere with my freedom to choose my own friends.

It is said that the elimination of racial segregation will mean miscegenation on a grand scale. This is the grand-daddy of all red herrings. Apart from the fact that its roots lie in a pride of race and blood that belongs properly to the Nazi, not to the Christian, philosophy of life, this sophism assumes that with the elimination of segregation there will be an end to freedom of choice in the matter of marriage. It conjures up in the minds of frightened mothers the fantastic image of thousands of screaming girls being carried off triumphantly to undesired marriage beds. Or if this be denied, then it must be admitted that it conjures up the image of thousands of delighted girls rushing happily into marriage with Negro boys. If the former image is fantastic, the latter image is hardly flattering to white boys; or, for that matter, to Negro girls.

The fact is, of course, that it takes two to make a marriage and that we have the right to marry whom we choose. Again, it is not the opponent of segregation, but its advocate, who questions this right. The racial pattern says to me: "I deny your right to marry anyone of Negro ancestry. If you violate this taboo, society will mobilize the full force of social ostracism to punish you for your transgression."

Those who are fond of raising the specter of miscegenation will say that I have unfairly represented their position. They will say that all they mean to affirm is that if the racial bars which now separate them are let down, whites and Negroes, as a result of familiar association, will lose their color consciousness and cases of intermarriage will multiply.

Nothing could better expose the artificial foundation of their entire position. It is they, not their opponents, who affirm that with the elimination of segregation intermarriage will become common. What is this but an explicit confession that race prejudice can only be kept alive by setting up artificial barriers which prevent white people from really knowing colored people? It is an admission that once the former are permitted really to know the latter they will immediately perceive the fallacy of racism. It is a frank avowal that the grand illusion of our racial superiority can only be maintained by manufactured social contrivances. It is to admit that prejudice inevitably dies once knowledge supplants ignorance. It is to recognize that segregation is not the necessary consequence of any *real* inferiority, but the artificial device whose function is to create the illusion of inferiority.

It is said that people have the right to protect the value and desirability of their homes by preventing undesirable characters from invading the neighborhood. The tattered shreds of this well-worn argument ill conceal the naked sophistry underneath. Like all the other analogies, it ignores the essential difference between *racial* segregation and other kinds of segregation. Granting, for the sake of argument, the right to keep moral delinquents or slovenly housekeepers out of the neighborhood, the question is: upon what ground do you refuse admittance to one who is neither a moral delinquent nor a slovenly housekeeper and whose only "offense" is that he has Negro ancestors? And the answer is: it is because you falsely and unjustly assume that the fact of Negro ancestry is itself a form of uncleanness. Establish your residential restrictions upon whatever other basis you choose—moral conduct, social grace, physical cleanliness, domestic propriety. (Whether or not the civil law will support them has nothing to do with the question at issue.) None of these restrictions implies the existence of a people whose nature is itself unclean.

The sophistry and hypocrisy of those who defend residential segregation by appealing to their right to maintain a proper standard of morals, of cleanliness, of beauty surrounding their homes is made manifest by the undoubted fact that these same people, for the most part, would prefer a white neighbor who violated all of their standards to a Negro neighbor who more than measured up to their most stringent demands.

A white debauchee will be admitted when a Negro saint would never be tolerated.

It is said that a school commits no injustice in refusing to admit those who cannot meet its intellectual or financial requirements. It is said that a school commits no injustice which says that it will not admit students who live west of Thirty-Second Street. *A pari,* so the argument runs, a school commits no injustice which says that it will admit only students not of Negro ancestry.

As in all the other analogies, the evasiveness is cheap, the sophistry transparent. Establish your intellectual, financial or geographical tests. It is the Negro who can pass every one of these tests except the *racial* test whose case exposes the essential difference and the essential injustice of *racial* segregation.

Do you or do you not believe that this is a race tainted and inferior *in nature,* so much so that any individual belonging to this race, whatever his personal qualifications, is by the fact of race alone rendered unfit to associate with those of other races? If you do not, then upon what ground do you exclude *this* Negro who can pass all your course examinations, who can pay his tuition, and who lives east of Thirty-Second Street? If you do, then you profess a doctrine which is branded as false by science, forbidden by the inspired word of God, condemned by the Vicar of Christ, and which, by denying that the Negro *as a human person* is fully equal to every other *human person,* violates a fundamental principle of justice.

There is another aspect of this which reveals unmistakably that segregation is not based, as the racist pretends, upon concern for purity of morals or physical cleanliness but upon the refusal to admit the equality of Negroes *as human persons.* The same person who will fight tooth and nail to prevent a Negro from living in his neighborhood will not hesitate to employ a Negro maid or a Negro cook. If he believes that Negroes are lacking in moral integrity, why does he permit a Negro maid to take care of his children? If he believes that Negroes are physically unclean, why does he permit the Negro cook to handle his food? The answer is obvious; he does not really believe either of these things; but he does believe that no one of Negro ancestry is his equal *as a human person.* To allow a Negro maid to bathe the baby or a Negro cook to handle the food implies no recognition of the equality of the Negro *as a human person*. But to allow a Negro to establish his home in the same neighborhood does imply a recognition of that equality and is therefore not to be tolerated.

It is for this same reason that many women who as babes were suckled by Negro mammies, who as children often took their meals in the kitchen at the same time with Negro mammies, as adults are outraged at the suggestion that any Negro should be permitted to dine, not at the same table, but in the same restaurant with them. The former experience implied no recognition of the equality of Negroes *as human persons*. The latter experience does.

It is difficult for the mind to emancipate itself from widely accepted social patterns. The history of the polemics about slavery provides a striking example of this. Today the Christian conscience instinctively repudiates slavery and without the necessity of recourse to involved casuistry recognizes it as incompatible with the dignity of man. Yet less than one hundred years ago the pattern of slavery was so woven into the social fabric that its protagonists found no trouble enlisting in its defense the support of many reputable moralists. The treatises they wrote make interesting reading today. One does not know whether to admire their ingenuity or pity their ingenuousness.

It is probable—at least we must think so if we are not to despair—that one hundred years from now the Christian conscience will repudiate with equal decisiveness the whole pattern of racial segregation. In that happy event the lucubrations of mid-twentieth century apologists for Jim Crow will make interesting, if sad, reading.

Meanwhile the mind, faced with a conflict between Christian principles and sound Christian instincts on the one hand and deeply rooted social prejudices on the other, ingeniously tailors the former to fit the latter. It is not always a conscious betrayal, although sometimes it is. The mind subconsciously—sometimes consciously—sows with rationalizations and evasions all approaches through which the imperative voice of principle might reach the center of conscience. After all, it really is easier to obey man rather than God. That is why most men are conformists.

The casuistical resources of the mind determined to conform to social patterns rather than to obey God are well-nigh inexhaustible. If nothing else will do the trick, the mind will simply affirm that black is white. There was the individual who was at no loss for an answer when, in condemnation of Jim Crow churches and Jim Crow schools, I quoted to him the categorical affirmation of the Pope that "Negroes have equal rights in the Church and must know that they have equal rights." With perfect aplomb he answered: "But what do you mean by *equal* rights?" I had no answer to that, just as I had no answer some years ago to the Buddhist monk whom I was attempting to persuade of the existence of a First Cause and who left me speechless and weaponless by blandly denying the principle of contradiction. There is no answer to a man who has at his command casuistical techniques which enable him to convince himself that by equal rights one means unequal rights. How is one to argue with a man who can prove that black is white, if not *simpliciter* at least *secundum quid?*

Then there is the moralist who, in discussing racial segregation, includes in his enumeration of the specific rights in justice which belong to all men whether "white . . . black, yellow or red" the "right to the pursuit of happiness, that is to say, to such equal opportunities as are required for the pursuit of happiness." And a few pages further on he blandly denies, without giving any supporting argument, that the exclusion of a Catholic Negro boy from a Catholic school is a violation of justice, provided that there is another Catholic school which will admit him.

How is the trick performed? It is easy: one forgets the principle of justice one has already admitted, looks the other way when the specter of *racial* segregation (the really pertinent point) looms up, and pretends that the only question at issue is the right to an education.

Yet none but the obtuse and insensitive can pretend for a moment that a people subject to a pattern of *racial* segregation enjoy equal opportunities with others for the pursuit of happiness. This pattern is a dark cloud over the happiness of every Negro who has not already been brutalized by subjection to the pattern. And the more sensitive the Negro, that is to say, the more he has succeeded in perfecting his personality (another fundamental right recognized by the moralists), the darker becomes that cloud. It is impossible to know Negroes without knowing this. It is impossible to look into the South without knowing this. It is impossible to put oneself imaginatively in the Negro's place without knowing this And if nothing else will do, it should be enough to read Richard Wright's autobiography to realize this.

One of the most naïve sophisms which the unavowed Catholic racist invokes to defend Jim Crow is the assertion that Catholic schools, since they are *institutions,* have the right to admit or exclude whomsoever they choose. It is a proof of the allure or sophistry that sincere men, themselves no friends of racism, have sometimes been beguiled by this far from subtle play on words.

Casuistry, properly understood and practiced, is a respectable and useful form of dialectics. It is the most widely accepted method of teaching the law. Its object is to develop facility in applying legal or moral principles to concrete cases. But it is precisely the kind of equivocation here manifested and whose purpose is to rationalize violations of principle that has brought casuistry into disrepute and given it its bad name.

In what sense is a Catholic institution a "private institution"? In the sense that it is not a state-supported or controlled institution. Therefore, should the state attempt to enforce a practice which violated Christian principles—as, for example, the practice of racial segregation—the Catholic institution is not obliged to submit; is obliged, on the contrary, to resist. In no sense is the Catholic institution a "private institution" *as against the Church,* regardless of what order or congregation or ecclesiastic authority directs it. Because it is a private institution, may it teach sexual promiscuity or birth control or hatred for one's neighbors? It is a *Catholic* institution and therefore under strict obligation to conform to Catholic principles. Among those principles is the uncompromising repudiation of racism in all its forms: "The *only* road to salvation is definitely to repudiate *all* pride of race and blood." (The words are those of Pope Pius XII; the italics are added.) If Jim Crow is not the natural offspring of pride of race and blood, whose offspring is it?

A lawyer friend of mine has pointed out that a logical extension of the argument from the "private" character of Catholic schools would be the contention that the prohibition by a state of Jim Crowism in public or private schools was an unconstitutional invasion of religious liberty. This would give us the bewildering paradox of a Catholic school defending, in the name of religious liberty, the right to defy the doctrines of the Church.

The mind which is bent upon defending racial segregation is inevitably forced to take refuge in equivocation, subterfuge, evasion and rationalization. The passages through which this leads are tortuous and labyrinthine and warp the logical processes of the mind. No conclusion which it reaches, however absurd, should be surprising.

There are other distressing features to be found in the discussions of this question which one hears among some Catholics. One would suppose that they were pagan Greek philosophers instead of Christian moralists. The argument nearly always proceeds in terms of natural ethics.

There are certain questions which these people need to be asked. Is the morality of human actions in no way affected by the fact of the Incarnation? Is every action which would have been permissible to a Greek permissible to a Christian? Does the supernatural have no bearing upon our moral actions? Does the Christian, by reason of the supernatural order and specifically because of the reality of the Mystical Body of Christ, have no obligations binding under pain of sin which he would not have in a natural order or in an order presumed to be natural? Is it proper for a Christian moralist to formulate his discussions in terms proper to Greek philosophy only?

It is curious that it does not seem to occur to such people that Christ's identification of Himself with every victim of injustice and uncharitableness has anything to do with the matter "Whatsoever you do unto one of these my least brethren you do unto Me." For the Christian who is not wholly dead to the real meaning and nature of Christianity these words give the complete and final answer to the race question. There is no need for statistics, no need for distinction and subdistinction. It is Christ Who is turned out of your school, out of your church, out of your hospital. It is Christ Who is ordered out of your restaurant, out of your neighborhood, out of your Pullman car. It is Christ Who is insulted, humiliated. Yet often it has been my experience in discussing the question with certain Christians that reference to these words of Christ is met with blank looks all around. There is an embarrassed pause such as would ensue were I to dunk my cake at a musical tea. I have evidently committed a dialectical *faux pas*. In the silence of the pause one can almost hear the minds behind the blank faces working. And they are all busy with the same thought: "Now whatever possessed him to introduce *that* irrelevant note into the discussion?" Then someone will clear his throat and quickly act to bring the discussion back to the solid ground of good sense: "Now whether you look at it from the point of view of communicative justice or distributive justice . . ." At that point for some curious reason I always think of Dostoevski's Grand Inquisitor."

"Whatsoever you do unto one of these my least brethren you do unto Me." Has this *fact* no impact upon the morality of Christian actions? Perhaps it could not affect the moral discussions of the Greeks, but surely the moral discussions of Christians cannot prescind from it.

The penalty exacted of those who do these things to Christ's "least brethren" was hell. It must seem rather pointless to them whether or not the Greeks could prove their actions no violations of strict justice in terms of natural ethics.

Perhaps most curious of all, however, is the common assumption that only justice imposes strict obligations upon the Christian conscience. So long as it is thought possible to prove that strict justice is not violated, it is assumed that any action is permitted to a Christian. Charity can recommend, but apparently it cannot oblige. It can recommend that the authorities of the Catholic school admit the Negro applicant. It cannot oblige.

This is a remarkable evacuation of the essential content of Christian morality. Sins against charity are sins and therefore immoral no less than are sins against justice. Christian morality does not *recommend* that we not offend against charity. It *obliges* us under pain of sin not to offend against charity. Many seem to suppose that charity is a work of supererogation, something that is nice to observe if we find it not inconvenient, but which we can ignore or directly wound with impunity if we choose to do so.

This fallacy is but one of the many consequences of the influence of the dehydrated moral notions of a capitalistic society which has substituted mere caricatures for the fullness of the Christian virtues. Instead of charity we have philanthropy: the rich man who with a lordly wave of the hand and an inner warmth of self-satisfaction bestows a generous alms upon the beggar. A nice gesture if he is capable of it, no sin if he is incapable of it.

It has been sufficiently proved that *racial* segregation violates strict justice. But the point here being made is that, even if justice were not violated, no one would pretend that charity is not grievously wounded. *Racial* segregation is certainly a sin against charity and, in the Christian dispensation, is certainly immoral and not to be tolerated. We can go to hell for sins against charity as easily as for sins against justice, perhaps more easily.

Death and Life

✶

JEAN C. DE MENASCE

REV. JEAN C. DE MENASCE *served as the director of a half dozen social workers' schools in postwar Italy and is one of the leaders of Catholic Action in Rome.*

✶

I HAD just been ordained a priest two weeks before and, faithful to the good advice that had been given me in the seminary, I was saying the next day's Office when the telephone rang and the housekeeper knocked on my door: "A sick call, Father." I jumped up from my chair, I took my brand new Ritual and it was so new that the newly printed pages still stuck together; I looked for the place, and my hands trembled with emotion. I found everything, I found the formula for blessing scapulars and Easter eggs, and then I found the right place and I hurried to the church. I had never before opened the tabernacle at night; it was dark in the church; I felt guilty as if I were a thief. It was the first time too that I had walked through the streets carrying Christ. The sick man lived in a dark little flat which gave onto the courtyard of a large building tenanted by clerks and workmen. It was in Rome. The concierge, a fat and jovial peasant woman, handed me the apartment keys. "He lives all alone up there," she said. "You can find your way, can't you, it's the end of a day and I don't want to climb all those stairs."

In the bed, which was not very big and yet filled almost the entire room, an old man—his face livid and the skin stretched tight over the bones—lay bolstered up on cushions taken from a sofa. After I had heard his confession and administered the Last Sacraments, I took off my surplice and I sat on a broken-down chair next to the bed. The electric light bulb that hung from the ceiling was broken and the only light came through the kitchen door. I tried to speak to him of God, of Paradise; he kept feebly nodding assent but spoke no word, and soon even this slight gesture of encouragement was denied me. He looked at me quietly, steadily, and two tears came very gently from his eyes. I said, "Be brave, be a man, you must not be frightened, God is not at all the way people describe Him, you must not cry." I did not dare stop talking, I kept on talking and talking. All the theological themes that I had been working on for my examinations at the Gregorian. I brought them up again one after the other: original sin, grace, the Incarnation, the Redemption, *de Deo uno et Trino*. The street sounds gradually had become distinct and now they broke the silence of the night. He was still looking straight at me and I did not dare stop talking and I did not dare leave him. At six in the morning the fat concierge opened the door. "Still here?" she said. "Yes," I said. "He has been crying and I did not dare leave him alone." The concierge walked over close to the bed and burst into laughter which was both motherly and jovial. "Ah, what a new little priest we have here; he does not even know when a man is dead. What do they teach you in the seminary?" She roared with laughter and she called in all the neighbors on the landing. Everybody crowded in and they all made fun of me and it was even entirely impossible to dress the dead man. I slipped out into the street and went back to the rectory.

A little Sister of the Poor who went all about the city giving hypodermics had found him. The Little Sister, who had also been a Great Lady, had hastened to the Cardinal: "What priest could go to see him?" she had asked. "His father is a terrible man, an unfrocked priest." And the Cardinal had smiled and had told her to telephone me.

The enormous and horrible building which housed the disfigured and mutilated wounded of the Great War stood behind the church of Saint John Lateran. The Sister had warned me: "If his father answers the doorbell he will shut the door in your face." That is exactly what happened but I was able to put my foot in the door. "Get out of here," roared a heavy-set man. He was surprised and furious. "I want to see your son," I said. "Go to the devil," he said. He pushed and I pushed, he swore and I swore. "Father, what's going on, what's all this noise?" a voice called. "Nothing; an impertinent fool wants to see you," the father called back. "Not at all," I shouted, "a priest wants to see you."

Out of breath, and embarrassed, I entered the room of the sick man, Captain Baby, as his friends had named him—men without faces, or without arms, or without legs, who lived with him in this building. "You want to try to convert me," he said. "Well, yes, if you put it that way, I do," I said. "Sit down and try," he said. Captain Baby was very young, hardly thirty years old. He had volunteered at the age of fifteen when he had learned that his father was an unfrocked priest. He had no faith, he had not even been baptized, yet he felt that a terrible humiliation weighed upon him. He had done everything to die; he had succeeded only in getting himself gassed and abominably mutilated in the woods of Bligny. "At most I've ten days more to live," he said. He told me these few events of his life between paroxysms of coughing: having practically no lungs left he was gradually turning almost black; his mother, gentle and massive, kept giving him oxygen. Just as a drunken man succeeds in walking straight only with infinite difficulty and at the price of an effort which exhausts him, so I tried clumsily, and embarrassed, to bring out all my school theses in apologetics. Captain Baby's education was on the primitive side; he believed all the old chestnuts, the Galileo business included, and Pope Joan. For three or four days between these paroxysms, which left him almost lifeless for hours on end, I kept answering, and explaining and laying down the law. Finally I said to him: "I'm through, I can't go on, I can't be schoolteacher and teach you the A-B-C of the Faith with you in such a condition; let me simply tell you what your death would be like if you were a Christian." And while I was speaking to him of Christian suffering conceived of as participation in and continuation of Christ's Passion, he interrupted me suddenly. "Do you think," he said "that the Cardinal

Vicar would be willing to ordain me a priest on my deathbed? I want to die a priest." His mother broke down sobbing. He had understood everything there is to understand.

On the morning of his Baptism and of his First Communion all those men in that house who had been abominably destroyed by the war were present; they were in the bedroom, in the narrow passageway, in the parlor and even in the kitchen; for several hours I heard confessions, after which Captain Baby and his comrades received Communion. His father was standing near the door. Captain Baby called to him, "Father, come here," and then he kissed the palm of his father's hands and then he called to me, "You too, Father," and I knelt down as I would before a newly ordained priest and kissed his hands. And that unhappy man who was his father went out from the room broken with love, broken with gentle love, humiliated and broken. The room was so filled with people that even I breathed with difficulty; a paroxysm came and the oxygen flowed down to the poor shreds of lungs that were still there. With a last trace of a smile Captain Baby said to me: "In spite of your Cardinal Vicar and your Canon Law I am offering Mass, my Mass, the Mass of my body."

The old peasant woman who sold eggs and vegetables to the Capuchins of San Lorenzo sent word that the woman who lived in the hut next to her farmhouse was dying of tuberculosis. It was only five o'clock in the evening but night was beginning to fall. It was raining hard. Sora Amelia was waiting for me under a tree. The man had thrown her out. "He wants to sleep," she said. "He would not even let me take the two children to our house for the night; he is mad at us because we bought a dog to stop him from stealing our chickens at night." I knocked on the door and getting no answer I entered the hut. Just as when certain fruits are overripe and yet remain bitter, the hut was stifling hot and the air in it was unbreathable, yet there were ice-cold draughts coming through holes in the roof and cracks in the walls. The little iron stove was red hot, the oil lamp threw strange and moving shadows over all the abominable disorder of the room. The whole family was lying on a bed which, Heaven knows why, did not collapse. With her cheeks ablaze and great eyes burning with fever, the dying woman was lying on the side of the bed which faced the door: on the other side of the bed, with his back turned, the man lay snoring. Between the two of them a little twelve-year-old girl stared at me with enormous frightened eyes. Across the foot of the bed slept the little boy. "I have come to say good evening," I said, "things aren't going very well, I'm afraid?" I sat down close to the bed; with the Blessed Sacrament close to my heart, I sat there trying to make friends. "Why don't you want to go to the hospital?" I said. But the woman obstinately refused: "I can get well here." I knew that there were only a few hours left for her to live. "Will you make your confession?" I asked. She shook her head. "I won't leave my man," she said. "It is he who pays the rent." Hour after hour I tried to make her understand that she would be leaving her man very soon and that she should ask God to forgive her for having abandoned her husband and her children. Her voice came out halting and whistling and she kept repeating over and over again with opinionated and idiotic stubbornness: "I don't regret anything; who would have paid my rent?" From time to time the man in the bed would snarl: "Get out of here and let me go to sleep: I'm not like you are, I do some work." And then I would say to the woman: "God is going to call you tonight from this house, it is time you thought about the other House," and then she would say: "I tell you that he is the man who pays the rent." Her poor little mind was like a moth attracted by a flame and it could not take leave of this tiny little idea which was the one thing that seemed settled and clear and which had formed the center of her miserable existence. Toward midnight she became incomprehensible, yet in those last sounds of hers I still could hear the words, "my rent, my rent." The man refused to get out of bed, refused to put the children out of the bed. The little girl had fallen asleep at the side of her dead mother. I was seized with a terrible nausea; I fled from the hut and leaned against a tree; I was sick at my stomach. Then I sat in the automobile and I cried as I had never cried since I had ceased to be a child.

The little Sister of the Poor who had taken me to Captain Baby brought me to a shabby little flat in the San Lorenzo district. "They are not married, they detest each other, sickness and poverty are the only masters of the house," she told me. A horrible looking hag with running eyes opened the door; she made no move to draw across her shrunken chest the filthy kimono that she wore. "May I see your husband?" I asked. "Perhaps that damnable Sister would not come back if I threw you out," she suggested. "Oh," I said, "I can assure you that we do not go in for that sort of bargaining." The sick man's bed was clean and neatly made up; I saw that the little Sister had been at work. The sick man said: "I don't want anything, I want to die in peace, it's not because I am poor that you can bully me." I tried to talk with him and to joke; I had some American cigarettes, "Vatican cigarettes." I went back often to see him but always he insulted me and jeered at me. He showed a sort of evil joy when he blasphemed. He did not blaspheme at all the way the poor devils I knew blasphemed, "not any more than I have to, and only when it is necessary, Father." One morning the Sister telephoned me that he was in a coma. His eyes were shut, he was drooling from his half-open mouth. The Sister kept wiping his mouth while the hag, in her eternal kimono, moved about between the bed and the kitchen. Only the hands of the dying man were in motion. Slowly, he lifted them up and then brought them downward in a solemn gesture. The woman began to laugh, but she laughed as if terrorized. She looked at the man in bed and she said: "Ah, excommunicated that you are, this is a fine time to be saying Mass." And she turned to me and she said: "Don't tell me that you didn't know that he is an unfrocked priest. He and I met during the war." With expressionless face the dying man in his last agony again and again attempted this gesture of his which was the gesture a priest makes at the Offertory. I gave him conditional absolution.

Before becoming a priest I had known Molina, the technician. This austere scientist, a gentle and quiet man, was the very type of the virtuous and atheistic anticlerical formed by the nineteenth century. One morning his daughter telephoned to me: "Father is dying; of course no one here believes in God but I wonder if it would not be well for Father to see a priest; he knows that he is very ill—just come to see him as if you were paying a call." "Good afternoon, Father, how clerical dress has changed you, I'm very happy indeed to see you, sit down I beg you and let me offer you a cup of coffee—as for me, it's forbidden," was Molina's greeting. We started in talking of this and of that, and, from time to time—at first only occasionally, but later very often—the engineer made mistakes, called me by the names of former colleagues of his, and once he even addressed me as "Your Excellency." And while he spoke, his voice also began to change, and it became harsh and vulgar. Before our conversation was ended he had become completely insane; he howled and fought and scratched at his wife and at his daughter. The two women stood there shuddering with horror. This man who had always been gentle and grave, who had made their happiness for thirty years, and who deserved to die the death of a wise man, had become a violent lunatic. His madness persisted until he fell into a coma. Not without a feeling of humiliation I asked his wife and his daughter if they would authorize me to give him Extreme Unction: "Since God could not reach him through his intelligence, perhaps God wishes to reach him in his madness." I had gone to a corner of the room, I was reading my Breviary, the two women in tears were busy with all those thousand necessary nothings which serve to help women in their grief. Toward four o'clock in the morning Molina drew himself up in bed and in his real voice, his voice of the past, a clear, friendly, cultivated voice, he said: "Elvira, Elvira, God exists." Then he fell back dead upon his bed.

"Since mother's death he is hardly recognizable, he seems to be going mad, he hardly ever goes out of the house, he has even attempted suicide," his sister said. And when I saw him he said: "Don't waste your time on me, I am lost, one cannot be a Christian if one has no love for anyone, for anyone at all." There were no tears in his eyes and he looked at me coldly. I said: "But you loved your mother, therefore you love someone; all that is necessary is to begin to love, and then all that is necessary is to continue to love." He said to me: "Very well, then, you force me to tell you; I have never told it to any of the family, but the fact is that I did not love my mother. I tell you that I did not love her, that I do not love her. When she died I went out of the room, I went out into the street, I went to the prostitutes, I stayed with women for hours and then I went to a good restaurant and I ate and I ate for more than a hundred lire. Do you hear me, do you understand what I am telling you, I bought myself a meal like the kind you buy when you get through your examinations." And I said to him: "You see how right I was, you see that you loved her so much that your nerves got all tangled up, the whole switchboard got tangled up; instead of crying, you went out and stuffed yourself; don't be an idiot, you can see perfectly well that you loved her."

The man, the boy, burst into tears, he cried as only a man can cry, with his arms, his back, and all his body. Through the tears you could see his real visage again, and the evil mask that had covered it falling away. He cried and he laughed with happiness. "Do you say," he said, "that I love my mother and that I love God? Are you ready to swear it's true?"

I said: "I swear it."

Patience of the Poor

GEORGES BERNANOS

GEORGES BERNANOS *is best known in the United States as the author of* The Diary of a Country Priest, The Star of Satan, *and* A Diary of My Times.

I BELIEVE that the world will be saved by the Poor, and indeed by that very species of the Poor which the world looks upon as incurable, which the world suspects of having been born proof against the Virgilian "cursed greed for gold," just as goats are proof against tuberculosis. Such Poor exist, of course, but we know little about them, if only because they know very little about themselves. In no sense have they taken vows of poverty; rather God has taken these vows in their place, without their knowledge; He has made sieves of their hands so that they can hold onto nothing.

We should be deeply mistaken were we to confound these people with spenders, with wasters, with the careless. The very sign of their mysterious vocation is not that they scorn money—in fact they sometimes get to the point of thinking that they love money as much as the rest of us. But if they do love money, they do not truly desire it; rather they dream about it, and we may well wonder whether they believe in it any more seriously than children believe in ogres and fairies. God keeps them in this state of innocent curiosity regarding that monster whose thirst could not be quenched by all the blood of the human race. I say that such Poor will save the world. And they will save it without wishing to; they will ask for nothing in return, simply because they will be unaware of the value of the service they will have rendered. They will carry out this stupendous task, and they will not win a farthing in reward. They will continue just as before to argue with the drugstore proprietor, the baker, the grocer, the landlord; they will continue each month to go through their financial sleight-of-hand and high strategy; they will bend their every energy to state with precision problems more absurd than that of squaring the circle; and, imagining that they are solving them, they will waste their time thinking them solved—dreaming, for instance, that they pay their debts, that, as they themselves would put it, they are "starting off on the right foot" at last. Unfortunately this is the sort of foot they never have, and what is more they get along very well without it, for they have no real urge to run too fast after fortune. They do not want money for today; they prefer to hope that it will come tomorrow, or the day after tomorrow, and it is this hope which is what they really love.

Hope. That is the word I have been wanting to get to. The rest of the world desires, covets, demands, requires, and the world calls all these things hope because it has neither patience nor insight nor honor; all it wants is pleasure, and pleasure cannot be awaited, hoped for, in the true sense of the word; waiting for pleasure cannot be described as any form of hope, but rather of frenzy, of agony.

Moreover the modern world lives much too fast, the world no longer has time for hope, the inner life of modern man in our days has too quick a rhythm to allow the formation and ripening of so burning and tender a feeling; the modern man shrugs his shoulders at the very idea of so chaste a betrothal to the future. The world no longer has time to hope, or to love, or to dream. Rather it is the poor who hope in the world's place, exactly as the saints love and expiate for all of us. The tradition of hope lies in the hands of the poor, just as the ancient lace-makers of Bruges have a secret technique which mechanical processes will never succeed in imitating.

You may answer me that the Poor, since they needs must live on hope, have not much more merit in hoping than in living. True enough! You might even add that the harder their life becomes, the more they should hope by way of compensation. Do you believe that the labors of these busy honey bees, the honey which seeps from their hives, might possibly be lost forever? O! certainly, no one really asks himself this question, since the earth is still possessed by the masters of modern industrialism. But the day will come—is not that day already near at hand? Do you not feel upon your forehead, upon your hands, the first freshness of its dawn?—the day will come when those who now, as though hypnotized, chase after their pitiless masters, the bloodthirsty masters who lavish human life as though it were some worthless raw material, who stuff their furnaces and their forges with human lives . . . when those who chase thereafter will stop short upon the road which leads nowhere. . . . Well, then, the word of God shall perhaps be accomplished; the Poor shall possess the earth, simply because they will not have lost the habit of hope in a world of the hopeless.

I realize perfectly that such an hypothesis will seem trifling to realistic political thinkers. "Whoever controls the whole of public opinion truly possesses the earth," they will answer me, "and since the Poor will never have enough money to control the first, they will never possess the second."

Yes, yes, you think that you are the masters of all public opinion, but you have only explored that part of public opinion which is most ready to your hand. You have summoned the peoples to profit, as you are now calling them to arms, and the squirming and grimacing multitudes have hidden the horizon from your eyes; their cries have filled, covered, submerged the silence of millions. But now you must act. You realists have promised the liquidation of a society whereof, moreover, you brashly wasted the resources, and silly fools are still trying to figure out the profits of such an operation, whereas you yourselves already know that all it will do is leave us a tremendous capital debt. So now you must create something.

We have seen you proudly boasting of a philosophy of man which attributes to this biped but one motive power—self-interest—but one god—force—and but one inner urge—instinct. We shall learn by experience what this philosophy is worth. Deign, realists, to understand me; don't take all this as some trifling witticism. You have been able to tear down a society, but you will never build up a new one with men formed after your pattern. To build is always a task of love. Sooner or later you shall have to make an appeal to a humanity which you do not know at all well, that you even refuse to know, because its existence would make your theses crumble, a humanity which is not realist in the meaning you give to the word. Another humanity, another species of men, who you believe will never demand anything, because they do not need the same things as you do.

Perhaps they will demand nothing; perhaps they will draw up no list of grievances. But—and mark my word—you will never get the best of their patience, of their holy patience. Whatever you knock down, they will rebuild behind your back—they will do it once, ten times, a hundred times. Tirelessly they will pick up everything that you have let fall, and they will hand it back to you, with a smile. The picture of life which you paint in your own mind is so gross that you believe you have found in violence the ultimate secret of domination, whereas experience daily teaches us that the humble patience of man has constantly, and through millennia without number, put in check the wild forces of evil. When you believe that you have beaten everything down, enslaved everything, you will still not have triumphed over the patience of Jesus Christ. "The patience of the Poor shall not perish, forever."

"What language you want?" Rico asked. "I speak Italian, German, Portuguese, English and French. Always bad accent, except in Italian. In Italian, I speak like a Roman. But in the others. I have a bad accent. You correct me when I make a mistake."

Then he went on to prove his claim. We were passing Mussolini's old residence and he pointed it out in each of the five languages, with a flowery little anti-fascist speech right out of the guidebooks.

I was full of questions right away. How long did he go to school? Where had he learned all these languages? And where on God's green earth did he pick up that awful speech—and in five languages, too!

Rico was quite willing to talk about things other than Mussolini's old balcony. He had quit school six years ago, when he was ten. He learned English from British and American fliers; German from the Nazis in Rome before the Allies arrived there; Portuguese from Brazilian pilots, his first Allied friends; and French from living near Paris with an American bomber outfit during the war and after.

The guidebook speeches were a new accomplishment. "I buy books about Rome and study them," he said. "Sometimes I go without eating all day so I can buy these books. But after I know them by heart" (the phrase surprised me, but soon I realized that his English vocabulary was naturally idiomatic, and, I suppose, so was his French, Portuguese and German) "then I can be a real guide. So far I don't know much. Just the first twenty pages. It's the same book in all these languages. So I learn the first part in Italian and then in the other languages. I take it page by page."

The first twenty pages covered the prison where Saint Paul was held captive, the Coliseum, the Roman Forum, the baths where Cleopatra cavorted ("you know, Vivien Leigh," Rico explained) and a brief description of the old Appian Way. At the catacombs of San Callisto, Rico was finally left with no more speeches to give.

"Next week," he said, "I'll learn about this. All I know now is that a man named Giovanni Battista de Rossi discovered it. But I don't know when."

Rico was more himself after the speeches ran out. We arrived at the catacombs about one o'clock, during the Italian siesta. There was a sign saying that visitors would have to wait until two-thirty to be shown around. So we waited outside in the carriage.

While we waited, the old man fed first his horse and then himself. He had a bottle of wine with him and a couple of huge meat sandwiches, which he offered to share with us. We refused politely.

"I knew you wouldn't take any," Rico said. "Americans are more dainty. They always think about whether things are clean. And you see that the old man is dirty. Don't worry, though. The old man doesn't care. He knew that you wouldn't take any. This old man is eighty-five years old. He started to be a driver when he was fifteen. He knows everything. And he had twenty-two children. How you like that—twenty-two kids! Not in America, huh?"

Twenty-two, I agreed, were a lot of kids.

"My father," Rico said, "had twenty kids, but they're not all living. And he's even now only forty."

His father, he said, sold rosaries and cameos outside St. Peter's, in the great square.

"Too many kids," Rico said. "Not for me. I'll have three, maybe four, but that's all. I'll be like the Americans. But not yet for a long time, though. Not until I'm thirty-five. Then I marry a beautiful wife, only eighteen. I come back to Italy for her. I don't want to marry American woman. But my Italian girl, when she goes to the States with me, she'll be like Rita after while."

Rita, I learned, was Rita Hayworth, who is Rico's favorite. He had just seen *Gilda* and, standing outside the doors that led down to the tombs of martyrs, he sang "Put the Blame on Mame, Boys," in an exaggerated but worshipful imitation of the Hayworth style.

"Rita, Rita," he said, rolling the r's, "Rita and America—that's for me, boys."

"What's the matter with Rome?" I asked him. "Here you are in the most wonderful city in the world and you want to leave it. Why?"

"I tell you," Rico said. "The first thing that's wrong with Rome is that it's in Italy. In Italy, there's too much rich and poor stuff. Not just because of the war, but always. Always it's that way. My father, he knows, he tells me. The rich people, they don't want the poor people to come up. They want the poor people to stay poor. Not like the States. Here, nobody cares if the poor kids don't go to school. The rich people, they rather have their cup of tea, trying to be like Englishmen, than give a poor kid something to eat. All over Rome and every other city in Italy there are kids with no place to live but out on the street. Do the rich people care? No. You go to the Bristol-Bernini New Year's Eve. Look at the rich people there. Fancy clothes from Paris and lots of champagne. What if a little kid came in and asked for something to eat: would they give it to him? No. They'd make the man at the door throw him out on the street again. They'd say, why doesn't he work? Even when he's only seven years old, why doesn't he work? Little kids don't work in the States, do they? Kids there aren't hungry all the time. So they don't steal so much. It's better when you have kids to be in the States."

I told him there was poverty in the States, plenty of it.

"Yes," he said, "but not like here. You know kids in the States with no mama, no papa, just sleep on the streets and eat what other poor people give them?"

"What else is wrong with Rome?" I asked him.

"Two more big things. First, the Pope is here. That means too many churches, not enough good time—like in Paris and the States. I'm Catholic like all Italians, but I don't like to live where the Pope is until I get to heaven. Second, everything is old stuff. Like the catacombs here. I'm sick of old stuff. I want new stuff. That's why I like the States. All new stuff. I'm new, so I want new stuff. The old man here, he's old stuff himself. For him, old stuff is good enough."

He told this in Italian to the old man, who thought it was a fine joke.

I asked Rico how he expected to get to the States.

"Don't worry," he said. "I'll get there. First, I save fifty thousand lire and while I'm saving I keep learning English, to get rid of the accent. Then I go to the captain of a freighter. Look, I say, here's fifty thousand lire. You take me with you. Let me work my way to the States. After I get there, you forget me. The first captain says no. So do twenty more. But one day a captain likes fifty thousand lire very much. He says yes. So I go to the States. When I get there, I make out. Don't worry, I make out. Since I'm a little kid eight years old, I learn many things. I'm not American high-school boy. I'm Hank. Take care of myself since I'm little kid. With Nazis, Fascists, Partisans, English, G.I.'s, Brazilians, even Frenchmen—always I know how to take care of myself."

"Let's see," I said, "when the war started you were about six years old. What happened to you until now?"

So Rico told his story, and while he talked he brought out finger-marked snapshots from a thick wallet to show me what he looked like as he was growing up. Until the first snaps of him, neat and tidy in a G.I. uniform, taken by American soldiers, appeared, he looked like a ragged little character out of *Shoeshine*. Every picture taken since the Americans left shows a maturer, handsomer Rico, growing ever better dressed, looking ever more poised.

"First I remember," he said, "it is still Il Duce and my father is selling cameos at San Pietro, like now. Only then he don't have so many kids as now. Those days I don't remember so good. Too much happen since. But I remember I go to a good school. It is called Fra Angelico. Before I am ten, I quit a couple of times and then go back. But ten years old I quit for good. I know how to read and write. That's enough, I think. Maybe not for you. For me, that's enough.

"Then I remember that my father is arrested and is sent to jail by the Fascists. Mama cries all the time, and we are very poor. There's not enough for all the kids, so I leave Rome. I get on a train that goes to Napoli. When the man comes for tickets, I hide in the toilet. And finally I get off at Napoli.

"I am only a little kid, and I am hungry and scared. So I go up to another kid my age. He is shining shoes in the station there. I tell him that I am hungry, and he says here's polish and a brush, shine shoes like him. So I do that in the station. We get money to eat, that kid and I, and right away we're friends. At night we sleep in a doorway together with other shoeshine boys. All this time I am getting to learn things. Especially how to take care of myself. And I'm mad about my father in jail, so I say I'm going to fight with the Partisans. I'm only a little kid, but I really believe I can fight with the Partisans. Finally, with my friend, I find the Partisans in the mountains. It takes many days, and all the time we're learning new things. After we get there, the Partisans say run along, little babies, you're no good for us. But first they give us something to eat.

"Then, after that, I come back to Rome. My mama cry, I remember, and is happy because I am not dead. For a little while I go back to school again. But we are always getting poorer and poorer, and even now there is a new baby. So I start to beg on the street. This is when I start to hate the Germans. They are in Rome then. When I say please give me some bread, they say, go away, dirty kid. And sometimes they spit. Even when I get Italian women for them (I'm not a pimp no more—that was when I was a little kid), even then they don't give me nothing.

"After the war when I am in Germany with my American major, I get even. Then I smoke Lucky Strike cigarettes and when the Germans ask me for butts, I say wait a minute. They wait, and then I stamp on the cigarette with my heel. Remember when you were in Rome—I say in German."

There was a snapshot of little Rico standing by a plane with some swarthy aviators.

"This is when I'm first mascot with the Brazilian squadron. I come to their camp one day after I leave Rome again, and I say can I be your mascot. They say okay, kid, you clean the barracks and you can eat here. For a long time I stay with them. That's when I learn Portuguese. Those Brazilians are good guys. Listen, here's one of their songs."

And he sang a sultry South American love song in Portuguese.

"But then after a while the Brazilians go away and they say I can't go with them. Then an English squadron comes to the same place. They say I can be their mascot but I must say always No, sir, and Yes, sir, and Please, sir—even to privates. They're a little like Germans, those English. But I stay with them, and I start to learn English. The English soldiers, they call me Henry.

"Finally an American squadron moves across the road. These guys I like better. So one day I ask them can I be their mascot. They say what's the matter, Hank, don't you like the Limies? I say, oh, just so-so. Okay, the American major says, come with us if you like to.

"The English major is mad when I tell him. Why you want to go with the Yanks? he says. Better guys, Major, I say. That's a mean thing to say, I know, but I'm only a kid then. I don't know better. All right, the British major says, get the hell out of here and don't come back.

"So I stay with that squadron, the Americans. The major says he has a boy like me at home. That's why he likes me. He takes me everywhere he goes. That's how I go to France and Germany. . . . Here are my friends in that squadron."

There were a dozen snaps of young Air Force soldiers; Rico usually posed solemnly at their sides.

"After the war, I come back to my family in Rome. Papa is back selling cameos at San Pietro now, and there are more babies. So I don't live at home. I live with some other black-market boys in an apartment. I speak good English by this time, so they let me work on the black market even though I'm still a kid. But I make more money being a guide. Like today."

The story took a long time. A priest appeared from somewhere and announced that the catacombs were open for pilgrims. It was almost two-thirty.

"I wait outside," Rico said. "I see them a hundred times already."

In the restaurant, later in the afternoon, Rico, who had talked so freely of his past, fell into the frankest kind of Walter Mitty day-dreaming about his future. It was then that it hit me hard that he was only sixteen.

"I see myself coming back from America after a couple of years. Just a visit, of course. I am rich and I have a big car. I walk into the house and give my father a big pile of money, American money. Here you are, Dad, I say, now you don't have to work no more.

"Then I go to the American Express. When the black-market boys come up to me, I put my nose up in the air and say, like a real American, Sorry, not enough. I look at them like I feel sorry for them. Too bad, I say, you're not American. Too bad. But everybody can't be American. Anyway, here's a Lucky Strike. Now don't bother me no more. I'm busy. I got to cash lots of money and then take airplane for New York. I have date with Rita at big night club. . . . That's me. That's Hank, the American. You wait and see."

The next morning I was scheduled for a papal audience. Somehow Rico found out about it. As I left the papal palace and came into St. Peter's Square, there was Rico waiting for me.

"Good morning," he said. "Now you saw the Pope. What's left? Today I don't charge you anything. We're friends now. You want to have coffee with me, and then we go to the Vatican Museum together, huh? Two times a week I go there and study the statues so I can learn to be a real guide."

So we spent a few hours in the museum, with Rico carefully writing down every little scrap of information I could give him about the art there, which information, I must admit, didn't amount to much.

After we left there, we strolled back to St. Peter's Square.

"I'm going into San Pietro," I said. "Want to come along?"

"No," Rico said, "I can't. Only on Sunday. The Swiss Guard at the door won't let me in, especially if he sees me with you. He knows me and he knows I try to be guide for English-speaking people. But I have no permit to be guide. So he told me I can't come to San Pietro, only on Sunday for Mass. . . . I leave you now. But someday I see you in America."

The last I saw of Rico he was walking out of St. Peter's Square on his way to get the bus for the Piazza di Spagna. He waved to me as I entered the great church.

That Suffer Persecution . . .

JACQUES MARITAIN

JACQUES MARITAIN, *the internationally known philosopher, is the author of many works, including* True Humanism, The Degrees of Knowledge, Freedom in the Modern World, *and* Creative Intuition in Art and Poetry.

BLESSED are they that suffer persecution for justice' sake: for theirs is the kingdom of heaven." The eighth beatitude confirms all the others (*est firmitas quaedam omnium beatitudinum,* says Saint Thomas Aquinas) and corresponds to the first; the circle of the Gospel's blessedness, which begins with the poor in spirit, is completed with the persecuted. They are placed under the same banner: theirs is the kingdom of heaven, *ipsorum est,* not precisely a possession to which they have a right, but something much more intimate, inward and personal—for a thing which is *mine* is within me as though belonging to me, more beloved to my heart than is my very self. He, the Poor Man, the persecuted above all who have suffered persecution, is not He, Himself, likewise the kingdom of heaven? He tells them that He is their treasure.

Those who suffer persecution for justice' sake. We know approximately, or we believe we know, what persecution is. But "for justice' sake"—there we feel the presence of a mystery. What is this justice for the sake of which they are persecuted?

The saints know what is this justice. They are persecuted for the sake of the justice which makes us adopted sons of God and participants in His life through grace; they are persecuted for the sake of the divine truth to which they bear witness and of that Word which was made flesh and came to dwell in the world and "His own received Him not"; they are persecuted for the sake of Jesus Who is our justice. "Blessed are ye when they shall revile you and persecute you and speak all that is evil against you, untruly, for My sake: be glad and rejoice, for your reward is very great in heaven. For so they persecuted the prophets that were before you."

Blessed are the saints. They know wherefor they suffer. Not only do they suffer for justice' "sake" but "for" justice, which they know and which they love and which they will. Throughout their worst sufferings and their darkest nights they are well satisfied to be persecuted, they know that persecution is good for them, they desire it as they might desire an earthly paradise, they are astonished and worried when persecution is lacking to them. But never do they lack it long. Saint Paul reassures them and tells them that all those who seek to live piously in Christ Jesus will suffer persecution. When they are persecuted they have obtained that which they have wanted, they have that blessedness of the Gospel for which they have asked, they are well served.

And when they die abandoned and persecuted, the Holy Ghost Who is called the Consoler reminds them in the depths of their hearts of all the things which their Savior has told to those who are His, and that same Spirit places before the eyes of their souls the image of Him who has opened the way for them and who has loved them first of all, even unto giving His life for them upon that cross of redemption to the partaking of which He has now invited them.

The saints are not the only ones to be persecuted. And the inner justice of the soul is not the only justice for the sake of which men suffer persecution. All those who have sought justice within the earthly community and who have suffered for its sake imprisonment or exile or death, and who, moreover, have been looked upon as fools or bad citizens, have not been offered the promise of the eighth beatitude for such things. The immediate object of their thirst, the immediate cause of their sufferings is not to conform themselves to the Savior who makes man just and holy in the eyes of God; it is rather the imperfect and obstructed labor whereby a little more human justice is introduced into the world. They have battled against the oppression or enslavement in which men have been held by men of another race, another nation, another caste or another class; they have battled with human means and for human ideas; they have very often had to have recourse to force against force, to appeal to the wrath of those who have been humiliated and downtrodden. On occasion their passion for earthly justice has been fevered by hatred and violence, or else led astray by great illusions which made them dream of constructing a Jerusalem of peace without God, or else bemused by a despairing revolt against both Creator and creation. At times they have sought to be titans, at times "grand inquisitors" like the one in Dostoevski's tale. Unhappy are those who seek for justice in this world and suffer persecution for its sake. To have done so is not sufficient to assure them of the promise of the kingdom of heaven. And the justice they seek and for the sake of which they suffer, they usually see rejected by men throughout the length of their struggle for it, and betrayed by men at the very moment when justice is able to go freely among men.

Nonetheless they also have obtained that which they wanted. For they have labored in time and under the law of time for a thing of the earth and an idea entrusted to history. Time will bring them their reward when they are no longer, their labor and their trouble will bear their own fruits on earth under forms which they themselves had not foreseen, bemused as they were in the eddies of the vast stream of history. I do not mean to say that every effort on behalf of justice automatically succeeds in producing an effect in the history of mankind; I am not so optimistic. To my mind everything depends upon the depth at which the thirst after justice and the suffering on behalf of justice—however mixed these may be—have been brought into life within the secret substance of a heart and of a spirit. If a man's actions, before having been given outward manifestation, have thus been given birth in the very depths of the spirit, they will equally take their place in the depths of history, and there they will go their shadowy way until one day a few of the seeds they contain come to take root and bear fruit among men.

Having granted this, it is clear that if we look upon things in themselves, there is neither separateness nor conflict between thirst after the justice of God's kingdom and thirst after justice in this sad world. The one summons the other. The latter threatens to drive a man out of his mind unless it is accompanied by the former; the former requires and awakens and sanctifies the latter. How could men who daily ask that the will of the Father be done on earth as it is in heaven not thirst after justice on earth and within the human community? How could men who believe in the Gospel as far as eternal life is concerned not believe in it for life here below—how could they resign themselves to men's earthly hope therein being disappointed? So long as abysmal poverty and slavery and injustice exist in the lives of men and in their moral societies, there will be no rest for the Christian. He knows that his God suffers in the persons of all those who are suffering, all those who are spurned, all those who are persecuted throughout the world.

Hence blessed is he who suffers persecution for the sake of the justice of God's kingdom and for the sake of justice on earth. He suffers abuse for Christ's sake when he is abused for the sake of his brethren. Blessed is he if he is doubly persecuted. The more unhappiness he bears in his temporal existence because of his desire for justice in temporal society and because of his undertaking to "ransom the evil of the days," the more utterly and the more surely is he persecuted; and the more may he consequently hope, if he is faithful, to have in life everlasting, which for the just begins even here below, the blessedness of the persecuted; the more can he hope that his is the kingdom of heaven.

In our own day we have seen monstrous persecutions, persecutions in which hangmen beyond number scientifically organized cruelty and assassination, bending themselves to the task of debasing man in his body and in his soul, not striking down persons condemned by reason of a faith to which at least they gave witness, but masses of men and women guilty only of the fact of their existence and wiped out like rats. And we have been able to verify the truth of the saying that next to the hangman what men despise most is his victim. Confronted by these great herds of victims left to their fate, the Christian questions his heart and even his faith.

He thinks of his Jewish brethren, of the ancient olive tree with some of its branches broken, among which he has been grafted. Six million Jews have been *liquidated* in Europe. Other masses of human beings have been deliberately exterminated, also in millions, in Poland, in the briefly conquered Russian provinces, in Serbia, and this in the name of "living space" or through political vengeance. These men and women have been put to death because they were hated in their quality as people and because others desired to wipe their race from the face of the earth. This animal hatred possessed supernatural eyes. In truth it was their very election, it was Moses and the prophets who were persecuted in them, it was the Savior sprung from them against whom the grudge was held. It was the dignity of Israel, within which the Catholic Church prays God to have all nations enter, which was buffeted in these despised wretches treated like the vermin of the earth. It was our God who was slapped and scourged in His fleshly lineage, before being persecuted openly in His Church. How strangely knowing a hatred, more aware than the weak love of our own hearts: even before that day foretold by Saint Paul, when church and synagogue would be reconciled, and which would be for the world like from the dead, they have been reunited in this devilish hatred. Just as Christianity was hated because of its Jewish origins, Israel was hated because of its belief in original sin and in the redemption and because of Christian pity, all of which had their source in Israel. As has been pointed out with deep truth by the Jewish writer, Maurice Samuel, it was not because the Jews killed Christ but rather because they gave Christ to the world that Hitlerian anti-Semitism in its rage dragged the Jews along all the roads of Europe, through filth and blood, tore from their mothers children from thenceforth not even possessed of a name, undertook to dedicate an entire race to despair.

Thus it happened that unwitting Israel has been pursued by the same hatred which also and first of all pursued Jesus Christ. Its Messiah shaped Israel to His own likeness in suffering and humiliation before shaping it, one day, to His likeness in glory. Such are the bloody implications of that fullness of Israel of which Christians, if they think in their hearts, can detect the precursory signs in the sequence of abominable events remembrance of which will ever be burning and yet which are already being pushed into the dungeons of indifference in the hearts of those who survive. Like ill-assorted fellow travelers, Jews and Christians have together journeyed along the road to Calvary. The great mysterious fact is that the sufferings of Israel have more and more distinctly taken on the shape of the cross.

But could they have any knowledge of this, all these innocent people struck down like pariahs? Blessed are they that suffer persecution . . . these words were not for them, were not yet for them, at least on this earth. They knew not that they suffered persecution for the sake of the Just Man sprung from Jesse's tree and from a daughter of Israel full of grace; they knew not of what "receiving," of what reintegration—wherein the kingdom of heaven would be within reach of their people—the persecution they suffered was the hidden tidings.

At least they did know that they were dying because of their people's vocation and because their people's passion for justice on earth is hated by the world. At least those of them who cherished in their hearts the spirit of prayer and the religion of the Scriptures must have known that they were dying for the hope which is Israel's.

The Christian, however, thinks of other abandoned beings whose lot awakens in the soul an unbearable anguish because of the unrelieved darkness of the night in which death struck them. I do not refer to those who throughout Europe languished in prisons and concentration camps, were shot down as hostages, perished under torture, because they had resolved not to bend their heads to the conqueror: such men and women knew why they were suffering and why they were dying. They chose to fight and to resist, they gave their lives for freedom, for their countries, for human dignity. I am thinking rather of those poorer beings who had done nothing except their humble daily tasks, and upon whom in a flash death pounced like some wild beast. Sacrificed by the whims of war and of savagery, persecuted not for the sake of justice about which they were not even thinking, but for the sake of the innocent fact of their mere existence at an unlucky point in time and space. What are their sufferings and their death except the likeness and brief summary wherein we may see the sufferings of millions of poor wretches throughout the course of the centuries, shattered without defense by that great mechanism of pride and greed which is as old as humanity? The conquered who have been reduced to slavery, the untouchables, the classless, the slaves of all ages, the black men sold at auction by merchants of human flesh, women and children laboring in sweatshops, the workers of the industrial age, all those whom abject misery has stripped of their human condition, all the people damned by the worldly community.

Certain events which took place during the course of the last war serve as terrible illustrations of what I am attempting to say. Let us remember the slaughtered people of the village of Lidice, the women and children machine-gunned and burned alive at Oradour on Corpus Christi, those peasants of the Vercors whom the SS, seeking vengeance for the fighting achievements of the underground, suddenly seized in their peaceful homes and hung head downward, encouraging dogs to tear at their faces. Let us remember others who by every artifice were induced to die in despair, for instance by hanging them just a little above the level of the ground so that they would jump continuously until their strength failed them and the hangman's rope strangled mere shreds and tatters of a human being. Let us remember those Jews overwhelmed with weariness, who after weeks of bloody journeying, would upon arrival at Buchenwald of their own accord lay themselves upon the shelves in the crematorium; let us remember the miserable wretches who were starved to death in sealed railway carriages. Where lay the consolation of these persecuted innocents? And how many others died completely abandoned and alone. They did not give their lives, their lives were taken from them, and under the shadow of horror. They suffered without having wanted to suffer. They did not know why they died. Those who know why they die are greatly privileged.

It all seems to take place as though the passion and death of Jesus were something divinely vast, that it must be shared by men in its various and contrasting aspects in order that some picture of that passion might be available to its members and in order that men might completely participate in this great treasure of love and of blood. The saints of their own wills enter into Christ's passion, by offering themselves along with Him, by knowing the secrets of the divine life, by living in their souls their union with Him, by putting into action, in the depths of their being, the gifts they have received. In any torture of the body or of the spirit, in the abysses of utter abandonment, they are still privileged people. That beatitude addressed to the persecuted illumines their earthly existence. The more they are abandoned, the more can they say with John of the Cross: "Mine are the heavens and mine is the earth, mine are men, the just are mine and mine are the sinners; the angels are mine and the Mother of God and all things are mine; and God Himself is mine and exists for me. What then, O my soul, dost thou ask and dost thou seek? All this is thine and everything exists for thee. . . ."

But those wholly and completely forsaken, the victims of the night, those who die as though they were the outcasts of earthly existence, those who are hurled into Christ's death agony without knowing it and against their wills—all these are making manifest another aspect of that same agony, and surely all aspects must be made manifest. Jesus gave His life because He willed it. But He likewise "hath made sin for us"; He was "made a curse for us, for it is written: cursed is everyone that hangeth on a tree"; He was abandoned by God on His cross of misery, without protection against suffering, without help against those who persecuted Him. (*Summa Theol.* III.47.3) As though a legacy left to His saints, He said *into thy hands I commend My spirit.* And as though a legacy left to another flock, He said: *My God, My God, why hast Thou forsaken me?* The great flock of the truly destitute, of those dead without consolation—would He not take care of those who bear this mark of His agony? How could it happen that their very abandonment itself would not serve as the signature of their belonging to the crucified Savior and having a supreme title to His mercy? In the throes of death, in the moment when they pass to the other side of the veil and the soul is on the point of leaving a flesh for which the world had no use, is there not yet time enough to say to them: Thou shalt be with *Me* in paradise? For them there are no signs, for them hope is stripped as bare as they are themselves; for them, to the bitter end, nothing, even from the direction of God, has shone forth in men's eyes. It is in the invisible world, beyond everything earthly, that the kingdom of God is given to these persecuted ones, and that everything becomes theirs.

On Modern Intolerance

JAMES N. VAUGHAN

JAMES N. VAUGHAN *served for several years as a director of* The Commonweal *and for a short period as its drama critic. He is now a practicing attorney in New York.*

A GENERATION ago Monsignor Ryan collaborated with Moorhouse F. X. Millar, S.J., on a volume entitled *The State and the Church,* in which he stated his views on religious toleration. Now [1941], with Francis J. Boland, he has restated them in *Catholic Principles of Politics* and they prove to be unchanged.

He starts with the idea that it is obligatory upon the state publicly to profess religion in some degree. In its highest development this obligation is fulfilled by profession of the true religion. Since the true religion is the Catholic religion, the conclusion is reached that every state in a soundly organized world ought to profess the Catholic religion. The world, however, is not soundly organized, for it is not formed of Catholic states. In truth there does not exist today any specifically Catholic state. Consequently the obligation to profess the Catholic religion stands in abeyance in respect of all modern states. Specifically in 1941 it is inoperative in respect of the United States of America.

Existing facts are perishing facts. Catholic states have existed in the past. They may exist again. If this should come to pass, the state would be morally bound to profess Catholicism. The outcome of such profession would not be a theocracy. Also ruled out would be the relationship between church and state in which the church would exist as a subordinate agency of the state on the English or prerevolutionary Russian model. In an ideal union occurring in a Catholic state the Church would stand to the state somewhat as the United States stands with reference to the several states of the Union: each would be autonomous in its own sphere. The jurisdiction of each would be restricted, but within their respective limits each would be sovereign. Delicate problems of adjustment would no doubt arise, but in principle they would furnish no obstacle to a workable union.

Suppose a church-state union of the ideal type consummated in the United States. Of the many questions arising from such a change one stands out as supremely important. If the state recognizes and professes the Catholic religion, can the existence of nonbelievers be tolerated? Monsignor Ryan says that the unbaptized and those born into a non-Catholic sect can never be coerced into the Catholic Church. Existence in their errors is to be permitted. They are also to be allowed to practice their several forms of worship if they do this "within the family, or in such an inconspicuous manner as to be an occasion neither of scandal nor of perversion to the faithful." And what of propaganda in favor of their several species of untruths? "This," says Monsignor Ryan, "could become a source of injury, a positive menace, to the religious welfare of true believers. Against such an evil they have a right of protection by the Catholic state. On the one hand, this propaganda is harmful to the citizens and contrary to public welfare; on the other hand, it is not among the natural rights of propagandists. Rights are merely means to rational ends. Since no rational end is promoted by the dissemination of false doctrine, there exists no right to indulge in this practice."

It comes to this: Catholics today are a minority in this country; this country also has a Constitution which Catholics as well as non-Catholics are bound in conscience to uphold; this Constitution bars profession of Catholicism as the state religion. While these three conditions obtain Catholics cannot pretend to prohibit free circulation of non-Catholic religious doctrine. But make Catholics into an overwhelming majority, remove the constitutional barrier and get state recognition of Catholicism, and doctrinal intolerance in the degree indicated above may follow without violence being done to anybody's legitimate rights. The reason why Catholics can promise intolerance when they shall have become a majority while demanding tolerance for themselves so long as they remain a minority is that "error has not the same rights as truth." Whoever defends "the principle of toleration for all varieties of religious opinion [must] assume either that all religions are equally true or that the true cannot be distinguished from the false." In these words Monsignor Ryan answers him who is disposed to murmur against his conclusions as harsh and illiberal.

The object of intolerance, Monsignor Ryan has said, is to prevent perversion of the faithful. We may add that the best of men—and the worst—have defended this notion. Intolerance is a kind of policeman for authority. Like blinders on a horse, it acts to keep eyes on the road untroubled by the pleasures or terrors of the wayside. It makes for unity, order and monotony. The principle of intolerance goes far beyond the question of religious orthodoxy. It weeds gardens, tames wild animals, corrects unruly children, rationalizes industries and suppresses crime. It beats down or tears up, it eliminates or sterilizes, it burns or mutilates whatever tends to mar unity, whether it be the unity, for example, of a garden, a family, a business, a nation or a religion. Intolerance considered with reference to human society and belief proceeds on the basis that there exists a definite plan, a definite belief or a definite policy. Its function is to forbid the proposal of any amendment to the plan, any doubt to the belief or any discussion in respect of the policy. Manifestly it is noncreative. In a benign mood it takes doubters, critics, dissenters, debaters and agitators into protective custody. When irritated it is more at home with whip, rack, gallows, guillotine and the stake. Intolerance accompanies success and efficiency in the world of action. It is the producer and conservator of likemindedness, which in turn is the source of all effective social action.

If man's vocation were to be merely a sheep, the case for intolerance would be perfectly unassailable. If man were designed to sacrifice individual existence in favor of the social whole, again the case for intolerance would be convincing. If ends could justify means, the case for intolerance would look good. If actions prompted by fears of disaster were necessarily holy actions, intolerance would carry the day. If dissent were always immorality, intolerance once more would sweep the board. It is the unhappy and historical fact that of the billions of men who have lived and died on this starved and blood-drenched earth only a trifling minority has constantly known the delights of a rich, secure and free existence. Men have in fact been handled as sheep, sacrificed to the social organism, employed as slaves in the service of the powerful and governed by gnawing anxieties as to the dangers inherent in dissent and social change. Intolerance has accordingly ruled the world, save for rare brief intervals. It is the subjective equivalent of war and it is no less widely distributed in time and space.

He would be a foolish, ridiculous man, wholly lacking in common sense, who would come forward with the idea that everywhere and at all times and in all situations intolerance is bad. No one in authority could long rule unless he could bend the human will to the ends to be served by authority. The problem of tolerance is a study in reconciliation of the permanent opposition between liberty and authority. A late example of how the issue arises in a concrete way is supplied by the opinion of the Supreme Court of the United States delivered on June 3, 1940, in the case of Minersville School Dist. v. Gobitis (84 L. Ed. 993). The Commonwealth of Pennsylvania exacts participation of school children in the ceremony of saluting our flag as a condition of attendance at Pennsylvania public schools. Parents are also by law of Pennsylvania required to see to it that their children attend school. For those lacking substantial means, obedience to the latter law involves attendance by their children at public schools. In practice this means the children of the majority are obliged to participate in the flag ceremony. Children reared in the Sect of Jehovah's Witnesses are taught to believe that the flag ceremony is forbidden by scripture. To them to salute is to worship a false God. The question became this: Could Pennsylvania properly force these children to participate in an exercise they regarded as irreligious or could the children, claiming the protection of the constitutional guarantee of freedom of religion, insist on toleration by the school authorities of their non-participation in the flag ceremony? This is plainly a problem in toleration, formed by categories of constitutional law. Deciding against the children the majority of the Supreme Court, speaking by Mr. Justice Frankfurter, said: "The ultimate foundation of a free society is the binding tie of cohesive sentiment." Saluting the flag, he said, is one agency for giving rise to that cohesive sentiment. To the objection that the ceremony should be exacted only of those who are not opposed to it on religious grounds, Justice Frankfurter said, ". . . an exemption might introduce elements of difficulty into the school discipline, *might cast doubts in the minds of the other children* which would themselves weaken the effect of the exercise. . . . A society which is dedicated to the preservation of these ultimate values [i.e., 'enjoyment of all freedom'] *may in self-protection utilize the educational process for inculcating those almost unconscious feelings which bind men together in a comprehending loyalty* . . . [italics supplied]."

With a little transposition these words of Mr. Justice Frankfurter could be easily used by Monsignor Ryan. They are words which remind one of Lunacharsky's program for Soviet education. "Instruction is not enough," he said. "Taken by itself it cannot form communists. Many men know Marx perfectly and nevertheless remain our worst enemies. It is necessary to educate *sentiment and will* in the communist direction [italics supplied]." Is the Nazi or Fascist theory of education any different?

The case for intolerance is implicit in these remarks. We must have a care that nothing shall be done or said which will occasion "perversion to the faithful." The people have a right to compel dissidents to conformity in action so that "doubts in the minds" of others shall not arise. The important thing is to educate "sentiment and will." What is this thing which perverts the faithful, produces doubts and alienates sentiment and will? Isn't man a *rational* animal? Aquinas said so. Is he not exclusively attracted to that which he deems *good?* Such was the opinion of Augustine. Does he not aspire to be *happy?* This, said Aristotle, is indeed his aim. This rational animal aspiring to be happy and drawn on solely by apparent good—can it be that there is also something painfully criminal in his composition? Why is it that all these rational, happiness-seeking animals do not agree on doctrine, on ritual and on valuations, in matters political, economic and, particularly, religious? Why do critics, heretics, dissenters and agitators exist? We all agree in ruling out the Manichean principle of diabolism in the explanation of the facts. (We agree on this, I mean, while discussing the matter in cold blood.) If diabolism is rejected, we must look for some other source not inconsistent with the essential traits of rationality, aspiration toward happiness and the ubiquitous incidence of the good with relation to every human action. I fear we are come to this: in partial explanation of dissent it must be conceded that those who disagree with us have *some* reason, *some* motivation which is not impure, *some* just grievance which leads them to dissent, drives them on to search for converts and supporters, and moves them toward organization of followers and institutionalization of their beliefs.

Dissenters and orthodox, moreover, do not always do their thinking with that pure and dispassionate intelligence which we may suppose is characteristic of the angels. Men have feelings, passions, interests, diseases, traditions and habits which fuse to form prisms by which the objective truth is refracted in ways corresponding to the peculiarities of the prisms. That which is received is received according to the nature of the recipient, as Aquinas said over and over and over again. I add: according, also, to his *second* nature, that is according to his momentary composition as a totality of capacities and experiences. Dissent is a permanent *datum* of human life, because the same thing is not seen by different men in the same way.

Dissent is being produced every minute of the day in some soul which has taken up a new perspective with respect to some body of orthodox doctrine or aspiration. It may also arise if not from a new perspective then from a new configuration of objective truth which has exhibited itself. Often dissent merely restates something asserted by others many times in the past. It may consist of an old error repeatedly refuted. (Nothing new under the sun; Acton said history was the struggle for mastery of about thirty ideas.) However that may be, the definitive suppression of dissent is impossible. It can be choked off for a time, but those charged to suffocate it will in the end relax their vigilance and dissent will be heard.

Monsignor Ryan, himself a brave, free and distinguished man, would be the last who would wish this to be otherwise. But for the indomitable man who can say *no* to prevailing beliefs and practices what ground would there be for optimistic expectations in respect to the numberless people who live today, exemplifying a faith and practice which all civilized men agree are in turn detestable lies or debased activities? The power of dissent is the power to purge corrupt society and to unmask lies; at the same time it is, of course, the power to sap the foundation of a good society and the power to create and propagate lies. But whether it is employed for good or bad objectives it cannot be uprooted from human nature.

Since the power is there to stay, it follows that like every other human power it is certain of exercise. If it is certain of exercise, the real question is, indeed, whether it is to be met, in principle, with force (intolerance) or patience (tolerance). This question, owing to its generality, admits of no complete answer. It is indispensable that the general question should be particularized if it is to be a satisfactory question. In respect of religion, for example, it would be useful to ask a question like this: In a Catholic state should a person having an official position equivalent to that now occupied by Bishop Manning be permitted to have a handsome church from the pulpit of which each Sunday he might deliver a sermon on what he deemed to be the errors in the doctrine of Petrine supremacy? That question makes sense. The answer to it should be *yes, by all means.* Let the Bishop Manning, Bishop Cannon, Dr. Searles or Rabbi de Sola Pool—even the Father Divine and Judge Rutherford—of the future Catholic state, wherever it shall be, preach when and where he can find a group to listen. And let the Catholics of that future day and state study what these preachers have to say. Catholicism will not lose its integrity and truth if it is removed from an *ex parte* basis. Suppose some Catholics are thereby lost? It is man's privilege, a privilege marking him off from all other animals, to be absurd, to be insane and to choose to be damned.

Examine carefully the thesis Monsignor Ryan feels obliged to uphold. The faithful are entitled, when strong enough, to be protected from the errors of their weaker contemporaries—the irreducible dissidents. The dissenters are to be driven underground. True, they are not to be coerced to come into the Church. But the authorities are to quarantine them as they do the carriers of a noxious disease. Why? Because those who are weak may be fatally attacked by the disease of untruth. Should life then be had without risk and without courage? Should the spiritual life of man know neither doubts nor temptations? Should man be shamefully born, hurriedly shrived, and brought half blind through this world accompanied by armed guards as if at the slightest jar his spirit, like fragile china, would shiver into worthless fragments? To save so poor a thing it would be impossible to justify the utterance of even a harsh word to the unbeliever.

Intolerance, the scabbard of war, ever demonstrates the bankruptcy of living, vibrant faith. It coincides inevitably with the withdrawal of men from relationships naturally generated by love, understanding and mutual respect. Its presence says that priests as such have ceased to talk and that the time has come to hear the voice of the politicians. Each group must close its frontiers. Inside the group, members whisper, shout or storm, each according to his genius telling himself and all other insiders what fine fellows they are. The outlander is pronounced barbaric, ignorant, vicious. As "everyone" knows he is a mere liar and cheat. When these things happen, where is the principle of divine love and pity? Where is the voice of reason? Where are patience, charity and justice? The principle of intolerance of erroneous religion propaganda in the life of the true religion is, in my judgment, a dangerous, unwarranted usurper of the authentic religious spirit which is tolerant on this subject.

Historical reason should be one of the main sources of any theory of tolerance. Looking to history, we readily see that intolerance has a legitimate function, since by its means effect is given to community law. But intolerance readily expands its claims until it seeks to compel the human mind to conform to one rigid type, or, hypocritically, to profess a conformity it does not in fact experience. Some limits, if only in the interests of common safety, must be imposed on intolerance. History is the source of these limits. It is no longer legitimate to approach the matter of intolerance solely on terms of formal logic. And it is the teaching of historical experience that, however perfect the *logical* case for intolerance, especially intolerance of religious propaganda, intolerance has been a principal author of the most deep-seated hatreds which have divided man from man and nation from nation. Only in very late times have forms of intolerance, closely related to politics, arisen capable of matching in fervor the hatred generated in the past by religious intolerance. The guaranty of religious freedom which finally gained place in the Constitution of this country was no child of logic. It was derived from historical understanding. But the gains made by historical understanding should be no less permanent than those achieved in the natural sciences. It is just as important to civilized life that men should believe in the doctrine of religious freedom as it is that they should believe that the earth is round. As the modern geographic idea on the shape of the earth adjusts itself to real fact, so also religious freedom, including the right to worship as one chooses and to propagate what one believes to be religious truth, adjusts itself to the historical facts of human life, thought and experience. History is strewn with the social shipwrecks of societies based on the principle of religious intolerance. Where such societies have not been destroyed they have tended to assume petrified forms and in the end to perish by way of desiccation.

God made man to be free; else men are only animals. Freedom is manhood. The area of human freedom should never be so narrowed as to make the fear of man's force and ostracism the substitute for self-responsibility and the fear of God which are alone the beginnings of all wisdom.

The Elect and Unwelcomed

C. G. PAULDING

C. G. PAULDING, *who served as managing editor of* The Commonweal *until 1948, was associated with the review* Esprit *in France and is now on the editorial staff of the* Reporter.

IN ANNECY, in France, in the days before the first war, the Catholic ladies of the upper classes went into mourning at the age of thirty for someone or other, dressed in black until they died, and then their daughters went into mourning, and so at Mass the church was always filled with ladies in black veils. Once a week the soldiers of the garrison paraded in the evening carrying torches through the streets; they played a march commemorating the aborigines of the region who had fought against Julius Caesar, and also *Partant pour la Syrie* because, as everyone knew, the Republic had nothing to do with the French Empire. In Annecy there was the convent of the Visitation which had been founded by Saint Jeanne de Chantal, the friend of Francois de Sales; there was also, at the end of the main street as you came to the lake, a statue, put up by the masons and the republicans, to Eugene Sue. To the Catholics of Annecy who were providing my early education it was as simple as that: on the one hand there was Saint Louis, King of France, the long and glorious line of French saints, the cathedrals, abbeys and convents; on the other hand there was Eugene Sue, a sub-product of Émile Zola who was interested almost entirely in excremental odors, and there was the Republic, interested mainly in closing convents, expelling monks, emptying the cathedrals.

The Republic, I was told, had been brought into existence by the monsters of the Revolution against the will of the "real France." The Revolution had led France into the "stupid nineteenth century" which had sprung from the abominable eighteenth century of Rousseau, Voltaire and the encyclopedists. The eighteenth had been made possible because Protestantism in the seventeenth had split France in two; the seventeenth, because, in the sixteenth, Rabelais had been irreverent and coarse. This process of following the thread of disorder and evil, as in a labyrinth, then stopped short; no attempt was made to explain why all this horror should have sprung so unnaturally, yet directly, from the great centuries of the Faith during which the Church had that full control of education which ever since it has sought to regain.

Péguy was living then and writing, Bloy was living and writing; neither of them was ever mentioned. What is more curious is the fact that the Catholic writers of the past were very little talked about. Pascal was difficult and dangerous, Bossuet, that immense and neglected mind, existed mainly because of his funeral orations over royalty and his connection with the revered monarchical past; the great Catholics of the past who possessed living interest for the Catholics of Annecy were Bonald and Joseph de Maistre, because no one has ever written more brilliantly against the revolution; all the subject matter of Bremond's great history of French spiritual writing was as if it did not exist.

As for contemporaries, a man who did not even pretend to be a Catholic took first place in their minds—Charles Maurras. Years later, in Paris, when I sat in a room in the Faubourg St. Germain and listened to this stone-deaf old man nothing had changed; I was invited by two extremely Catholic and pious ladies to meet the man "who still might save the Church and France"—assisted by his friend Léon Daudet.

Maurras did not speak about any Catholic writers; he spoke about the nineteenth century non-Catholic writers. Maurras said don't read them, any of them, don't bother to read them; they are all of them Republicans and stupid; read what Daudet says about them. He has a dirty nickname for each, he even tells how each one of them smells and who is syphilitic; read his *Hérédo*—syphilis as the source of genius. But even with Daudet be careful because he loves good writing, he has an objectionable fervor for the work of art which sometimes leads him to forget the party line. Daudet supports Proust.

Maritain was living in Meudon then, outside Paris where there were trees and from the garden you looked down on the Seine—writing and teaching; the young artists, the young philosophers from the schools came out to Meudon to see him . . . the two ladies sat in their tapestried room and served madeleines (Proust's), while the deaf old man poured out his hatred and contempt.

What is called the Catholic literary renaissance was in full swing. But it was only by accident that an American in France could find out anything about it. It was only by accident that a Frenchman in France could find out anything about it. The mass of French Catholics ignored it and still ignore it. The men who were and are making it were and are alone, isolated in a little world of their own. Bloy was alone in his poverty, Péguy, in his shop at the gates of the university, was alone with his little group of socialists—almost like a Trotskyite. Ernest Hello was so alone that no one read him. But it is not a question of whether or not these lonely Catholics were read; it is only that they felt themselves to be alone, neglected, deserted by their fellow Catholics, and said so again and again. Bloy said nothing else but that he was alone in the century, alone with the Bible and with justice, alone with the Jews and their providential destiny, speaking only to Christopher Columbus or Napoleon.

Under the circumstances, with the Catholic press, with Catholic critics, with the Catholic bourgeoisie busy with anything and everything except with the men of the Catholic renaissance (upon which they now are making their living) there could not be any such thing as a Catholic literary revival in the sense of a mass movement. What happens is that, from time to time, a few more Catholics than usual start reading authors they have long neglected or disliked. Then they boast about their discovery, often for political reasons and, because they are divided in their political opinions, they use the same rediscovered genius to further completely conflicting aims. That is what they did to Peguy. The man who was a socialist, who fought for Dreyfus (Catholics at the time said he fought against the army and the nation) and who died in combat against the Germans, was Vichy's idol and that of the Resistance—at the same time.

It remains true, no matter what inflated talk there is about a French Catholic renaissance and no matter how pumped up it is for political purposes ("we have always been more radical than the communists; read Saint John Chrysostom about the rich") that there is a disparity, spiritual and literary, between people like Paul Bourget, René Bazin—with the rest of the dismal and utilitarian list of popular writers enjoyed by Catholics—and men like Péguy and Bloy, which justifies the use of the word "renaissance" or of any other word strong enough to mark the difference. A great change indeed has taken place. What is the nature of this change?

French Catholics had always known that the great writing of the nineteenth century had been done by people who were not Catholics and who disliked Catholicism. They had spent their time trying to destroy these men. They had not spent their time trying to find out why these men and their books were so obviously important, why their influence had spread all over France, and why any historian of literature will always speak of them rather than of the Catholics who attacked them. There were these works in every field—poetry, the novel, history, philosophy—which stood out as the great works of the French nineteenth century and of the first part of the twentieth. The French Catholics interminably attacked them, or tried to forget and to persuade others to forget that they existed; or they nibbled at the edge of the century's achievement, standing round at deathbeds to claim for literary Catholicism men like Baudelaire and Rimbaud who had spent their lives saying no.

French Catholics had always known that, outside a definable and limited circle, the French people—most workmen and most peasants and most intellectuals—had accepted the Revolution and the Republic and had never accepted the Second Empire, or the Restoration. They had always known that the ideas of freedom and equality of opportunity —which mean under French historical circumstance free state education and the secular schools—were in France to stay. They had allowed the Catholic schools to remain schools for the upper and middle classes; they had spent their time trying to destroy the Republic.

The Republic and the achievement of the non-Catholic writers were not destroyed; the great change which came about in the minds of a certain number of French Catholics and which gave new life to Catholic thinking was this: they found out that the failure, on the intellectual and artistic plane, of contemporary French Catholicism was not due to the attacks made on Catholicism by Voltaire, Zola or Anatole France, but to the fact that French Catholics had not read Voltaire or Zola or Anatole France with any serious attempt to find out why they wrote as they did. On the political plane they discovered that the Republic's anti-Catholicism was made inevitable by Catholics obstinately refusing to show any real interest in seeking the new techniques of economic and social freedom without which the people of France felt and were enslaved. The Catholics found out that whenever one of them during the course of the century had made an effort in this direction, he had not been supported by Catholics, he had been rejected by Catholics, and that this was the reason why it was non-Catholic social thinking, that of Proudhon and the others, which was taken seriously while Catholic social thinking was not.

The great change came when a certain number of Catholics began to look directly at the subject matter, the realities of the life and art of modern times, rather than allow themselves to be diverted any longer by their perpetual criticism of the way non-Catholics had been looking at them.

That is, of course, the reason why non-Catholic Frenchmen started paying attention to these Catholics. When they found that Péguy was as serious as Zola about defending Dreyfus, as serious as any man living in his socialist convictions and in his solidarity with the workers, as serious as any freethinker (as any Catholic) in respecting his wife's refusal to become a Catholic, as serious in his devotion to Our Lady of Chartres as any of the kneeling figures on the sculptured portals of the cathedral—they found reasons to respect a Catholic. (He composed his *Cahiers de la Quinzaine,* he set his own type by hand, he worked the press—the socialist workmen in the presses of the Left Bank found reasons to respect him as a workman.) Léon Bloy was another man who was totally engaged in his work, the work of justice. He wasted an immense amount of time in his attacks on minor and forgotten personages in the literary world of his day, but he did so out of a sense of outraged justice, and, of the few people who knew him, a handful loved him, others hated him—his landlords must have thought him insane, just as he thought them possessed—but no one said he was having fun with his Catholicism. When Mauriac writes novels that are not tricked out with edifying conclusions, non-Catholic Frenchmen read his books and respect him because he respects his work and his own temperament.

But when you put them together, adding any others you care to add, Bernanos, Claudel, Francis Jammes, there are too few of them. Even if you go back and scrape the century to find a few more—but they are mostly forgotten, like Huysmans, or they are men like Barrès who was not really a Catholic writer (there is Verlaine if you like)—there are still too few of them. There are too few of them to count for very much.

They are all we have in France, they are more than we have anywhere else, they have done extraordinary things for a few people, their influence is extraordinarily greater than their numbers; it is active, perhaps growing, in France and outside France; it is an immense help to us in America, freeing many talents, directing many intelligences—yet it is hardly a renaissance, and we had better leave that word to the Italian and other large movements. If we are honest, we take the Catholic names and then, at random, names from the other list, that of non-Catholic nineteenth century French writers: Hugo, Flaubert, Zola, Rimbaud, Baudelaire, Mallarmé, Anatole France, Romain Rolland, Gide, Proust, Valéry. These lists do not balance; there is no argument at all; they just do not balance. And even in this pitiful aftermath of the war, with the French uncertain and close enough to despair, it is Sartre and Camus who are writing the books and the Catholics once again are in the role of critics.

You can say that one cry of love from Péguy, one image of Chartres like a great ship rising on the horizon of the plain of the Beauce, one cry of agony from Bloy, "the only sadness is that we are not Saints," weigh more, have a greater spiritual density than all of the non-Catholic work of the century put together. But then you can say, and it will be true also, that one prayer, one pure act of love, one accepted grief (because of man's interdependence outside all time and because of the doctrine of reversibility) serve mankind's salvation better than all the books, Catholic or not Catholic, that have ever been written. But we are discussing the Catholic claim to importance in contemporary literature and on that plane the lists do not balance.

I had no great luck with my education. The people in Annecy would walk me past the statue of Eugene Sue (there was an inkwell adorning it, I think) and that would turn the conversation to literature. They yet had to wait a short while, not being prophetic, before they could explain that Proust meant nothing, but as for the names already filling out the list which illustrates the nineteenth century, they said they were important, their evil influence had its importance, for the sole reason that the atheist schoolteachers taught everyone that they were important —actually, all of them were profoundly stupid: Catulle Mendès had an intolerably bad breath, Zola's death prefigured hell, they were no better than Presidents of the Republic or cabinet ministers, dying in water closets in a railroad station or after the manner of Felix Faure. But the stupidity theme was stronger than Daudet's scatological one and, anachronistically, the Annecy people preferred to think that all the great writers were simpletons—who fell out of trains, like President Deschanel.

Not one of the French Catholic writers or critics whom we now respect would talk like that today. That also is the great change.

It was not only by the French Catholics that I was advised not to read the important people of the century, that an attempt was made to deprive me of the texts necessary for an understanding of the world we live in. I received a letter from Hilaire Belloc, whom I admired and admire for his sonnets, a letter which I treasured and for which, later, I was never able to forgive him. In it, he rattled off the names of Marx, Hegel, Kant, Spinoza, together with those of a dozen more German writers and philosophers, including I think, Goethe, and advised me not to bother my head about any of them. To each name he added a single adjective, muddlehead, imbecile, bore, etc.; his mind, unlike Léon Daudet's, was clean, his adjectives bluff and hearty, but the arrogant system was the same: do not read them, I will give you all the necessary answers, and brightly too. Perhaps if I had not been traveling abroad I might have had a different and better early education.

Of course, all this is not just about France; it is not just a question as to whether or not there are good French Catholic writers or, if they exist, whether they constitute a renaissance, a revival or a side show; it is that Catholics, everywhere, in all nations, have been now for a hundred and fifty years (ever since the French Revolution) in a modern world—floundering about, accusing this or that century, blaming Calvin or Luther, Voltaire or Rousseau, or all of them together, of having brought about the ruin that surrounds us. And now it is the communists whom we accuse, but of course they too come directly from Rousseau.

Thus we have succumbed to a belief in a spiritual determinism, a counterpart of economic determinism. We admit a law of the filiation of evil; diligently we trace evil back from generation to generation, and then it all pours down again upon us, down through the centuries, on into the future, and we stand there, helplessly, watching it rattle like coal down the chute. What can we do, we say? There was that friend of Madame de Warens, and with one book he ruined society forever and ever. . . .

For a hundred and fifty years—I am speaking of the intellectual, political and artistic action of Catholics, not of their spiritual life—we have been constantly on the defensive in this modern secular world; we did not create trade unions (we talked all the time about the guilds of the thirteenth century), we did not write great novels (we talked about Dante), we opposed the liberation of peoples because theoretically they could only be free in a world which had ceased to exist—and when the democracies, in France, in Italy, arose against our will, we sulked and did not lead them. Catholics cannot have this retreat from the world, and pre-eminence in the world—not at the same time.

We have been absent because we have not looked at the problems with which the world presents us, we have been looking exclusively at what other people have done about them. We have been busy writing about what these other people have written—like professors, busy writing commentaries, like school teachers busy correcting papers, assigning marks. But French writers now, the first of Catholic writers to do so, are looking directly at the problems, at the central problems of justice and truth; French Catholics are writing directly about them, seeing them all for themselves, unassisted, without waiting for someone else to tell them they are there. They act on their own, they are unassisted—except by the existence of the inexhaustible reserves of French spiritual life created throughout the centuries, throughout all the centuries including the "stupid" nineteenth, upon which they, and all of us may draw. That is what they are doing; that is the whole meaning of the French Catholic literary whatever-you-call-it.

The Crime of Anti-Semitism

NICHOLAS A. BERDYAEV

NICHOLAS A. BERDYAEV, *the Russian philosopher and author of* The End of Our Time, The New Middle Ages, The Russian Idea *and other books, died in the spring of 1948 in exile near Paris.*

HOW would you feel if all the people you met never mentioned your father or mother except with the greatest disdain, if their attitude toward your parents was pure scorn and sarcasm? But that is what happens with our Lord Jesus Christ. We forget, or else do not wish to know, that our God Who became Man was a Jew by birth; that His Mother was a Jewess, the flower of the Jewish race; that the Apostles were Jews as well as all the prophets; and that our holy liturgy is gleaned from Jewish books. How can we express, then, the monstrous insult and blasphemy it is to demean the Jewish race?" These words by that ardent Catholic Léon Bloy were addressed particularly to Christian anti-Semites, who may well ponder them.

What a mysterious thing is the historical fate of Jewry! Its continued existence down through the centuries is rationally inexplicable. No other people of the world would have endured through such a history. Above all others the Jews are people of history: they introduced into human consciousness the very concept of the historical. And to this people history has been merciless. Theirs has been a long story of persecution and the denial of elemental human rights. And after this long history, demanding terrible intensity of effort for mere self-preservation, this people has still maintained its own, unique visage, a fact recognized all the world over, amidst all other peoples, and often cursed and hated. No other people in the world would have survived such long dispersion, without losing its identity and dissolving among other nations. But the inscrutable will of God is that this people should be preserved to the end of history.

It is permitted to each of us to have his sympathies and antipathies with regard to nations. Some people do not like Germans, or Poles, or Rumanians. There is nothing we can do in such a case; one cannot be constrained to love, and it is hard to suppress an instinctive dislike. But hatred for a whole people is a sin: it is equivalent to murder, and the hater must bear his own responsibility. As regards the Jews, the problem is specially complex. They cannot be considered simply a nationality: a whole series of the marks of a real nation are lacking in the Jews, while on the other hand they have qualities which other nations do not possess. The Jews are a people apart; theirs is a special, exclusively religious destiny. They are the chosen people of God, and this accounts for the tragedy in their historical lot. God's chosen people who gave birth to the Messiah and then rejected Him, cannot have a simple historical destiny like other peoples. This people is welded together in agelong unity, not by those qualities which usually consolidate and unite a people, but by its religious destiny alone. Their very creed compels Christians to recognize the divine election of the Jewish people, though Christians often forget this, or hesitate to accept it.

How strangely paradoxical is the fate of the Jews! The passionate longing for a temporal kingdom and the total lack of a state of their own, something granted even the least important of the other peoples of the world; the messianic consciousness of their own election met by scorn and persecution from all other people; refusal of the Cross as a sign of offense, and crucifixion throughout their whole history. This is perhaps the most surprising: those who refused the Cross have had to carry it, and those who accepted it have so often crucified others.

The real ideology of anti-Semitism is racial and this is the most widespread of all forms of hatred of the Jews. Germany is the classic center of this ideology which is to be traced in Luther, Fichte and Richard Wagner. This theory proclaims the Jews an inferior race, rejected by, and hostile to, all the rest of mankind. But strange to say, the inferior race appears to be the strongest, eternally victorious over other races in any free competition. This racial anti-Semitism is inacceptable to the Christian philosophy: it is irreconcilable with Christian universalism. The Nazi persecution of Catholics in Germany was due to the fact that Catholicism is universal. It was Christianity which proclaimed the truth that there is neither Greek nor Jew. Christianity is intended for all men and every man, regardless of his race, nationality, class or social position.

Neither racial anti-Semitism nor racism in general can withstand criticism from the religious, moral or scientific viewpoint. The Christian cannot accept such a theory, because he is obliged to see in every man the image and likeness of God. Racism is no more possible for a Christian than is nationalism. But even from the general humanitarian point of view racism is intolerable. It is inhuman, it denies the worth of the individual, the value of human personality. It permits personality to be treated as an enemy, to be destroyed if necessary. Racism is the coarsest form of materialism, far more crude than economic materialism. It is the extreme form of determinism, a denial of spiritual freedom, where representatives of the despised race are burdened with the curse of their breed, and for them there is no salvation.

Hatred of the Jews is often the search for a scapegoat. When men feel their personal misfortunes are bound up with those of history, they begin to look for someone on whom to lay the blame for it all. It is no high compliment to human nature, but man under such conditions finds relief and satisfaction if he can discover someone to hate and revenge himself upon, as the cause of all his woe. Nothing is easier than to convince people of a low degree of mentality that Jews are guilty of everything unpleasant. The emotional ground is always ready for planting the myth of a world-wide Jewish plot, or of the secret power of "Jewish Free-Masonry." When I meet people who think they see in the Jews or the Masons the party responsible for all their misfortunes and they ask me to agree with them, I always say: "It is very clear—you and I, all of us are the chiefly guilty ones." This seems to me the more truly Christian attitude. There is something degrading about the fact that those who in fear and hatred consider the Jews so powerful are thus labeling themselves as weaklings, incapable of holding their own in free competition with the Jews. The "Jewish question" is not only sinful and inhuman, it is evidence of serious weakness and incapacity.

We must consider one other charge against the Jews. They are accused of founding both capitalism and socialism. One might think that in both cases some credit for construction would be accorded to "Aryans"—we should not leave it all to the Jews—but according to these critics the Jews made all the scientific discoveries, were the only notable philosophers, created capital and industry, brought forth the world-wide movement of socialism with its struggle for justice and the amelioration of the status of the laboring class. In Jewish hands is the whole of public opinion, the press of the world and what else have you. I must admit that, as an Aryan, I find this attitude insulting, and I cannot agree to thus turning over everything to the Jews.

In the Middle Ages they were money-lenders, the only occupation they were permitted to follow. Thus Jews created the money-lender and the banker types, but they created as well the typical idealist, self-forgetfully devoted to an idea, poverty-stricken, and living only for nonmaterial interests. Now "Aryans" also gave a helping hand to the development and the exploitation of capitalism. European capitalism was born among the merchants of Florence. And usually those who accuse the Jews of creating capitalism are not themselves enemies of the system; they would merely like to be more successful in capitalist competition, to have more capital than the Jews.

On the other hand, the Jews are accused of being the creators of socialism and the principal actors in revolutionary social movements. This is not according to the facts. Lenin was not a Jew, neither were many other leaders of the Russion Revolution, neither were the great masses of workers and peasants who gained the victory for the revolution. Of course the Jews played a significant part both in the revolution and its preparation. In any revolution it is the oppressed who always play a large part—oppressed nationalities, or oppressed classes. The proletariat has always taken an active part in revolution. It is to the credit of the Jews that they have participated in the struggle for a more just social order. This charge against the Jews, however, finally amounts to the main accusation that they are trying to gain control of the whole world.

Such a charge would have some sense in the mouths of those who themselves were not striving for power and an ever mightier state. But "Aryans," and Aryans who are Christians, confessing a religion which recognizes a Kingdom not of this world, have always striven for worldly power, and have set up how many temporal kingdoms! While the Jews had no state of their own, not even the smallest, Christians have possessed mighty kingdoms, and have struggled for ever greater expansion and sovereignty.

Christians have been anti-Semites chiefly on religious grounds. They recognize the Jews as a race rejected and accursed, not because they belong to a lower form of humanity, hostile to all the rest of mankind, but because they rejected Christ. Religious anti-Semitism is essentially anti-Judaism, and anti-Talmudism. The Christian religion is in fact hostile to the Jewish religion as it was crystallized after the Jews had refused to recognize Christ as the expected Messiah. Judaism before Christ is something quite different from Judaism after Christ. There is something deeply paradoxical in the fact that the appearance of Christ on earth, the Incarnation, God becoming man, took place in the bosom of the Jewish people. For the Jews it was extremely difficult to accept the Incarnation—that was easier for the pagans. God becomes man—to the Jews this was blasphemy, infringing upon the greatness and transcendence of God. In the early Jewish conception God was constantly intervening in human life, even in its minutest details, but He never united or amalgamated with man, never took on human form.

Here is the abyss between Christian and Judaic concepts. Christianity is a religion of God-become-man, a trinitarian religion. Judaism is pure monotheism. The chief religious charges made by Jews against Christians is that Christianity is a betrayal of monotheism: instead of one God, there is the Trinity. Christians base their religion on the fact that a man appeared in history who called himself God, the Son of God. For the petrified concepts of Judaism that was blasphemy. Man cannot be God: he can be of the nature of God, a Messiah, but not God himself. And if he calls himself God, he cannot be the true Messiah. Here is the root of the world's greatest religious tragedy.

Ever since, throughout all Christian history, we hear the charge that the Jews crucified Christ. Ever since then, a curse lies upon Jewish people. The Jews called down curses on themselves, agreed that the blood of Christ should be upon them and upon their children. They took upon themselves the responsibility. The Jews crucified Christ, the Son of God, in whom the whole Christian world believes. This is the accusation. But Jews were the first to accept Christ. The Apostles were Jews. The first Christian community was Jewish. Why not praise the Jews for this? Jews cried "Crucify Him, crucify Him!" But all peoples, it seems, have had an irresistible tendency to crucify their prophets, their teachers and great men. Prophets have been stoned to death in all times and countries. The Greeks poisoned Socrates, the greatest of their sons: do we curse the Greek people for that?

And it was not only Jews who crucified Christ. Throughout all their long history, Christians, or those who call themselves Christians, have by their deeds crucified their Lord, crucified Him by their anti-Semitism, by their hatreds and their violence, by their service to the powers of this world, by their treason to or their distortion of the truths Christ taught. The "Aryans" also have rejected Christ, are rejecting Him every day. And they do this in the name of their own kingdom. It is nobler openly and directly to reject Christ than to use His name for the advancement of selfish interests. When we curse and persecute the Jews for having crucified our Lord, we take the attitude of family vengeance, an attitude common in many ancient peoples, among them the Jews. But the idea of blood feud is absolutely unacceptable to Christian consciousness. It goes quite against the Christian idea of personality, personal worth and personal responsibility. Christian principles admit of no vengeance whatever, personal or collective, as in a vendetta. The desire for revenge is sinful and demands repentance. Race, blood, vengeance—all these are foreign to true Christianity and came into it from ancient paganism.

Jacques Maritain, leader of French Thomism and defender of integral Christian humanism, has a notable article in the symposium *Les Juifs*. He presents the interesting idea of a diversity of missions. Christians have accepted the supernatural truth of Christianity, the truth about heaven, but have done very little to attain justice in the social life of men, have not applied their truth to society. The Jews, on the contrary, did not accept the supernatural truth of Christianity, but have been the bearers of truth about the earth, justice in human, social life. It is a fact that the idea of social justice was introduced into human thought chiefly by the Jews, while "Aryans" have more easily reconciled themselves to social injustice. In India there grew up the idea of caste, sanctioned by religion. In Greece the greatest philosophers never rose to the height of condemning slavery. The old Hebrew prophets were the first to preach Justice in human social relationships, the first to defend the poor and the oppressed. The Bible tells of periodical redivisions of wealth, so that riches should not be concentrated in a few hands, and that there should not be a sharp division between rich and poor.

To convert the Jews to Christianity it is very important that Christians themselves should be converted, should become real, and not merely formal Christians. Those who hate and persecute cannot be called Christians, no matter how many prayers they say. It is Christians themselves who offer the greatest obstacle to the conversion of the non-Christian East, India and China. The Christian world, with its wars, its national hatreds, its colonial politics, its oppression of the working classes, is a great stumbling block.

In the true Christianity of the future there will be no more "Christian states," which have been a falsification and distortion of Christianity. Christians will press on in the spiritual struggle and in consequence will regain the inner influence which they have lost, and will once more carry conviction. Above everything else it becomes Christians to defend right rather than might, and thus again they may blossom in this world. Christianity must defend human worth, the value of the human person, of every human individual, regardless of his race, nationality, class, or place in society. And it is against human personality, against the freedom of the human spirit, that attacks are now being launched from all sides. Among these is the anti-Semitic movement which denies human values and human rights to one part of humanity. The Jewish question is a test of Christian conscience and of the spiritual power of Christianity.

The Analyst and the Confessor

VICTOR WHITE

REV. VICTOR WHITE, O.P., *English psychologist and essayist, was formerly editor of the Dominican monthly,* Blackfriars.

WE ARE often assured by those who should know best that sacramental confession and psychological analysis[1] are very much the same thing. On this point at least there would seem to be a considerable measure of agreement between many Catholic spokesmen and many psychologists: if they differ, it is only in the assertion of the superiority of their own respective wares. While the psychologists will tell us that sacramental confession is a sort of naïve and undeveloped, prescientific forerunner of psychological analysis, it has become almost a commonplace among many Catholic apologists that analysis is a secularized and truncated form of sacramental confession.

The equation deserves somewhat more critical examination than it customarily receives. Doubtless there are certain superficial resemblances which might incline us to put them both into the same category, and

[1] I use this somewhat clumsy term rather than "psycho-analysis" lest I be thought to have in mind only Freudian analysis, of which alone the term "psycho-analysis" can strictly be used. By "psychological analysis" I understand any psychotherapy which employs depth-analysis, whether Freudian, Jungian, or any other.

it is probable that a more careful comparison of the two procedures may reveal still deeper affinities and connections between them than at first sight appear. But there are still more obvious and essential differences between them which cannot be overlooked without risk of great confusion both in theory and in practice. We have only to take a look at what actually takes place in the confessional and what actually takes place in the analyst's office to see that the differences, even on the surface, are very marked indeed; and a closer acquaintance with their respective aims and presuppositions will further widen the chasm that divides them. We shall soon learn that the analyst who plays the confessor will be as bad an analyst as the confessor who plays the analyst will be a bad confessor, and we shall be put on our guard against the dangerous type of apologetic which might be understood as offering the confessional as a substitute for psychotherapy: dangerous because of the disappointment it must arouse in those who know no better than to suppose it to be a cure for psychoneurosis, and the contempt it must arouse in those who do. Nothing but good, we believe, can come from a closer acquaintance by the analyst of the practice of the sacrament of penance, or by the confessor of the practice of analysis. But before we can hope to see how the one can illuminate, and perhaps subserve, the other, it is of the greatest importance to avoid all initial blurring of their basic differences. Here, as always, *distinguer pour unir* is the indispensable precondition for accurate thinking.

And the distinctions are indeed basic, as becomes evident as soon as we attempt to sort out and compare the constituent ingredients of sacramental confession with those of psychological analysis.

Few analysts, and those hardly the most trustworthy, would be prepared to present us with a formula which would cover all the component elements which go to make up an analysis. Just how an analysis will proceed, of what it will consist, what part in it will be taken by the analyst and what by the patient, what it will and will not achieve and what paths it will follow: none of these can be determined in advance. Its starting point, its development, its procedure and its term will alike be determined by the material which emerges in the analysis itself, by the patient's response and the analyst's skill. It is an adventure of exploration into uncharted territory: there may be compasses, but there are no ready-made maps. It is a medicine, but one for which there is no uniform prescription. The ingredients of which it is to be made will differ widely in every case, and will be dictated by the material itself and no a priori preconceptions. Indeed its therapeutic success will depend on nothing so much as on the ability of both analyst and analysant to rid themselves of predetermined plans and prejudices.

In striking contrast, thanks to centuries of actual practice and theological reflection, the ingredients of the sacrament of penance are neatly and definitely sorted out, formulated and tabulated. These ingredients, with their technical names, are familiar to most Catholics from their very catechisms. The instructed Catholic "going to confession" knows fairly exactly what will happen; what he has to do and what the confessor has to do. He is probably familiar with the traditional dissection of the sacrament of penance into its component parts: he knows that, like all the sacraments, it consists of certain definite "matter" and certain definite "form." He may not appreciate the logical and metaphysical considerations which have established this matter-form analogy as a technical device whereby theologians analyze the sacraments into their components; but at least he knows the authoritative character of its results. And he knows that the constituent elements of the sacrament of penance are thus authoritatively classified under three heads: (1) remote matter; (2) proximate matter; and (3) form. These may well serve us here as terms of comparison.

The "remote matter" of the sacrament of penance—that is to say, "what it is all about," the subject with which it is concerned, the material of which it is made and to which the "form" gives a specific "shape" or significance—is stated to be *the sins of the penitent committed since baptism.*

At once a striking contrast jumps to the eye when we turn to the counterpart of this "remote matter" in psychological analysis. Sin, truly, is an evil; and psychotherapy is also concerned, as is every therapy, with an evil. Moreover, both the sacrament and the analysis are concerned to remedy the evil. But the evil with which each is concerned is essentially different, even mutually opposed. Sin is defined as an evil human act; that is, a human activity which lacks the goodness and rightness it should have in conformity with divine law. In theological language it is *malum culpae,* "the evil men *do.*" It is, of its very nature as a human act, in some measure voluntary: and a sin is sinful in the precise measure in which it is willed. A psychoneurosis, on the contrary, is a certain *malum poenae*—an "evil men *suffer*" or "*undergo.*" It is a sickness, and as such something essentially involuntary, and usually contrary to the sufferer's will both in itself and in its symptoms and manifestations. It is something that *happens to* us, not something we *do;* though it may lead us to action, these actions are neurotic symptoms in the precise measure in which they are involuntary. We may say that while the sacrament of penance deals with certain evil results of human *freedom,* psychotherapy deals with certain results of human *compulsions:* with thoughts, feelings, emotions, conflicts, patterns of behavior which the patient "cannot help," which are uncontrollable by his will and usually clean contrary to it. Confession presupposes the power to sin and to turn from sin and seek forgiveness; analysis usually presupposes necessity and impotence and seeks liberation and freedom. In short: the primary and direct concern of the sacrament is with willful *misdeeds;* the primary and direct concern of analysis is with a certain kind of involuntary *misfortune.*

This difference is quite fundamental. Whatever resemblances may be found, we cannot overlook the essential difference in the material with which the sacrament of penance and any kind of psychotherapy are respectively concerned.

From this basic difference spring others which are hardly less striking. Sin, being essentially voluntary, is also essentially conscious, while it is of the very definition of any analytical psychotherapy that it is concerned, at least no less, with the unconscious. Sacramental confession, as we have already remarked, is concerned solely with actual sins committed after baptism: it is not concerned with inherited sin, whose remedy lies within the province of baptism itself. In contrast, psychotherapy cannot confine itself to factors acquired in the patient's own lifetime, still less limit itself to any definite date in the patient's history. It can on no account neglect inherited factors and dispositions; least of all can any depth-analysis which, under whatever name, recognizes a "collective unconscious" as an important factor in mental health and sickness.

The "proximate matter" of the sacrament of penance is the three acts on the part of the penitent: confession, contrition and satisfaction. Here we have three definite and deliberate acts, interiorly performed and exteriorly expressed, required of the penitent as a *sine qua non* constituent of the sacrament. Each represents a predetermined operation of mind or will in regard to the "remote matter." Confession implies conscious acknowledgment of that "remote matter," and its expression in words. Contrition implies the turning of the will *from* the same, and its turning *to* God and the divine will. Satisfaction, the willing acceptance and performance of some task imposed as compensation and as a token of good faith and willingness to accept the penal consequences of sin.

It is presumably in the first of these—the act of confessing—that the resemblances between sacramental confession and psychological analysis are more particularly supposed to lie.

But the "confession" required of the penitent and the "confession" required of the analysant are two very different things; and the difference lies in the difference of "remote matter" which we have already noted. What a penitent is expected to confess is very clearly defined and restricted to the sins committed since his baptism or his previous confession. No such limitation can bind the analysant. Though no analyst who knows his business will want to exclude such material, he will still less seek to limit his patient's "confessions" to his real or alleged misdeeds. And he will be concerned with them, not precisely as moral offenses, but as causes or symptoms of neurosis, and as providing—together with the patient's conscious or unconscious attitudes to them—important elements in the total picture of the personality with which he has to do. The patient's "good deeds" will interest him no less than his "bad" ones (confessors are notoriously, and rightly, impatient with rehearsals of the "penitent's" virtues!) while dreams, free associations, spontaneous reactions and other manifestations of the unconscious will interest him still more. His business is less with what the patient does than why he does it. Only from this totally different standpoint may there be some overlapping, but never complete identity, between sacramental and analytical "confession." The psychological processes demanded by each differ correspondingly: the former requires a certain concentration of conscious memory and the orderly recital of a selection of its contents; the second, contrariwise, a mental and physical relaxation which permits the free flow of uncontrolled phantasy and the suspension of regular "directed" mental activity. The uncomfortable confessional box with its hard kneeler, and the couch or armchair of the analyst's office, admirably express and promote the two very different kinds of "confession" for which each is appointed.

Psychological analysis knows nothing of contrition or satisfaction as predetermined acts to be required of the patient: it would fail entirely of its purpose were it to lay down in advance the conscious attitude which the analysant was to adopt to his material. This can no more be predetermined than can the material itself.

Still less is there any equivalent in psychological analysis to the *form* of the sacrament of penance. This "form" is the words of forgiveness pronounced by the priest: it is the specifying and determining element which makes the sacrament of penance to be what it is; it is the efficacious sign of reconciliation with God, and so the very remedy for the evil which is the sacrament's "remote matter." Nothing of the sort is to be found in psychological analysis. Some very superficial resemblance might be suspected in certain cases in which reconciliation is effected with some *imago* projected upon the analyst; but there will be no "remedy" except in so far as the transference is resolved, the projection withdrawn and assimilated to the patient's own conscious ego. There is still considerable disagreement among analysts as to what their own precise role in analysis should be. But few, even of those who most strongly advocate his "active" intervention in the process, would maintain that the ultimate remedy comes from the analyst rather than the analysant and his own response to his own material. None certainly would claim divine power and authority to forgive sin.

So the differences between sacramental confession as understood and practiced in the Catholic Church and psychological analysis as known and practiced today are considerable and profound. Are we then to conclude that there are no connections between them, and that they are so wholly diverse that they can hardly be spoken of in the same breath?

To say this would, we think, be a grave mistake. We may not overlook either the psychological value of sacramental confession or the "religious" features of many an analysis and the close connections which may be found between them. Here is a subject which deserves much more careful exploration and consideration than has yet been given it, or is possible in this brief essay. But once the essential differences between the two have been understood, we may offer a few suggestions as to where such exploration might profitably be directed.

It should be remembered that although *malum culpae* and *malum poenae,* sin and misfortune, are essentially different, and even opposite in their voluntariness and involuntariness respectively, there is a close causal link between them. It is elementary Christian teaching (and not only Christian) that the first is the ultimate cause of the second. Sin results in temporal (as well as eternal) punishments and consequences, and Saint Thomas Aquinas explains how the disorder and disharmony of man's psychological powers and activities is, more especially, the automatic outcome of sin (cf. *Summa Theol.* I-II.82.3 and 85.3). This must not be misunderstood in the sense of the cruel and unchristian assumption that all suffering, especially mental suffering, must be attributed to the sufferer's own personal and actual sins (such as constitute the "matter" of the sacrament of penance): we are forbidden straightway to ascribe it to the sins of "this man or his parents" (John 9:2). But it is true that original sin is the ultimate cause (by removing the original grace which was the cause of man's psychological integrity and harmony) of all such disorder, and that its perversity *can* be enhanced by personal, actual sin. It should further be remembered that not all such disorder (being quite "normal" in fallen human nature) can be characterized as pathological or neurotic. But psychology itself finds it increasingly difficult to eliminate moral disorder from the etiology of mental disorder. The materialistic and mechanistic belief that a neurosis could be diagnosed without consideration of the patient's ethical valuations or behavior, and that it could be "cured" without any moral response or alteration, is one which few psychologists today could be found to accept.

So while sacramental confession (including contrition and amendment) does not deal directly with psychoneurosis, we need not be surprised to find cases in which it is indirectly therapeutic: indirectly in so far as it may remove one of its causes. But it is perhaps as prevention rather than cure that sacramental confession, especially if practiced with regularity and with frank and unflinching self-examination, may serve the ends, if not of psychotherapy, then at least of mental hygiene and prophylaxis. Analytic experience witnesses to the very great extent to which unconsciousness of the "shadow" side of life contributes to the formation and persistence of neurotic complexes. A patient's failure to meet consciously and deliberately the challenges ("temptations" or "tests" in Catholic parlance) which life brings him, whether from his own character or his environment or their mutual impact; shady compromises, never fully faced, with life's conflicting demands; a consequent narcissistic idealization of ego and corresponding neglect of the less acceptable traits of his character: all these, notoriously, are a common breeding ground of neurosis. Frequent and honest self-examination, and the necessity of formulating its findings in the confessional, may alone do much to promote a more complete self-awareness, and to prevent these less pleasing features of a personality from sinking into unconsciousness, where alone they will generate neurotic symptoms. Hence, while sacramental confession is not ordained to cure, it may do much to prevent, the disorders with which psychotherapy is concerned. We say, "It may"; indeed it should. But other factors, inherited or environmental, may enter in to prevent its exercising this particular efficacy: and indeed in certain cases (notably those known to Catholics by the tragic symptoms of "scruples") it may increase rather than prevent the virulence of the disease.

On the other hand, while psychological analysis is not ordained to forgive sin, it may do much to free the patient from those compulsions which make both sin and repentance from sin—and even any clear-eyed self-examination—impossible.

It should also be remarked that, although psychological analysis cannot demand contrition of the patient, it is seldom successful unless it brings about something which, at very least, is not unlike it: a radical change of the patient's conscious outlook, a *metanoia* or change of mind, and with it of his moral valuations and behavior. It is a truism that if an analysis does not change the patient's outlook on life, his whole mentality in greater or less degree, it achieves nothing. The very enlargement of consciousness involves a shifting of his whole center of awareness, and with it of his standard of values. This change, however, is not something that he brings to analysis, but something which emerges from the process and its material themselves. Numerous case histories show striking resemblances not only between the results of analysis with those of religious and moral conversions, but also in the very symbols which eventually emerge from unconscious sources to induce the transformation. We may here recall C. G. Jung's celebrated declaration made in 1932: "During the past thirty years, people from all the civilized countries of the earth have consulted me. I have treated many hundreds of patients, the larger number being Protestants, a small number Jews, and not more than five or six believing Catholics. Among all my patients in the second half of life . . . there has not been one whose problem in the last resort was not that of finding a religious outlook on life. It is safe to say that every one of them fell ill because he had lost that which the living religions of every age had given to their followers, and none of them has been really healed who did not regain his religious outlook." He added that, "This, of course, has nothing to do with a particular creed or membership of a church"; but he has also called constant attention to the parallels between dream processes and their healing symbolism with those of recorded religious initiations, conversions and illuminations. He has also remarked on the similarities, both in their mode and in their results, of the healing factors and experiences in analysis with what religious belief holds to be the effects of the operations of divine grace. That they are such in fact we can never have sufficient grounds to affirm with certitude; but neither can we a priori deny the possibility. The actual facts (unfortunately mostly locked away in case histories) certainly deserve thorough examination. While man is limited to the appointed channels of grace and forgiveness, God is not so limited; and there seems to be no foregone reason why the theologian can deny to dream-symbolism the *ex opere operantis* efficacy he must allow to the sacraments of the Old Law, the baptism of John, the sacramentals of the Church or—it may be added—the dream symbols of the Scriptures. Though little can be affirmed or denied with certainty, the resemblances are sometimes too impressive to be totally ignored.

The most that can be said in summary is that although sacramental confession and psychological analysis are two wholly different things, pursuing two different but interrelated purposes; the purposes of the one may sometimes happen (*per accidens*) to be attained through the other. But when the prevention, or more rarely the cure, of psychoneurosis sometimes results from sacramental confession, this arises from the conscious human activities which it involves. If, however, divine grace and forgiveness are sometimes attained through the processes of psychological analysis, this can only be from the patient's response to God's uncovenanted mercies through the inner life of his soul.

Religion and Psychiatry

KARL STERN

DR. KARL STERN *is a practicing psychiatrist and the author of* The Pillar of Fire *and* The Third Revolution.

THERE have lately been a number of papers—for instance, Father Victor White's fine essays—dealing with the problem of integrating the psychoanalytic method with religious concepts. These discussions seem to make it necessary to consider another aspect of the problem—the philosophical superstructure of present-day psychology. As has been pointed out so frequently, psychotherapy and the philosophy "going with it" are two different things which must be examined separately; and this "philosophy" has a tremendous impact. Just as our cultural climate has been permeated by an atmosphere emanating from the biological scientism of the post-Darwinian period, and an economic scientism of the post-Marxian period, so it is now permeated by an ill-defined current which derives from the present-day psychological concept of man, particularly from psychoanalysis and from behaviorism. Moreover, those of us who work in the psychiatric field are daily confronted with the question of how one can reconcile the methods and observations of present-day psychiatry and social psychology with the moral concepts of the

Judaeo-Christian tradition. This sense of incongruity has assumed huge dimensions. Priests and ministers are beginning to attack psychiatry, particularly psychoanalysis, because of what they conceive to be an immanent destructive principle. Psychiatrists and psychoanalysts begin to question fundamental religious values because they find in them what they believe to be some sort of eternal well of neurosis. Many of them hold that, in the light of the discoveries in psychoanalysis and social and comparative psychology, the concept of God, the values of good and evil, should be re-examined, and the very mold of man ought to be recast. Indeed, it is no exaggeration to say that we are standing in the middle of what might be called a psychological revolution.

In order to analyze this, we might consider first the greatest exponent of this revolution, Freud himself, and the Freudian school. There is no doubt of the genius of Freud. Probably no single individual has contributed more to the knowledge of human psychology. The methods of psychoanalysis, when used properly, can offer remedy to suffering human beings. The psychoanalytical concepts (including those which were contributed by the derivative schools of Adler and Jung) have opened a field which is as beneficial to mankind as the introduction of anesthesia into surgery or the discovery of chemotherapy.

However, psychoanalysis is followed by a philosophical smoke trail which, although it can be dissociated from the method and its genuine results, has in reality an extremely penetrating power. In order to illustrate this, we must understand what Freud himself has to say. At one time, Freud, speaking about the early reaction to his ideas, said that he encountered a great initial resistance; we can understand this resistance only in terms of the *beleidigung,* the *offense,* which his ideas inflicted on mankind. He linked himself with two other "offenders" of earlier times who had inflicted a similar modification on man's status in the universe. There was first Copernicus. Until the time of Copernicus mankind had been living with a geocentric consciousness. The earth was in the center of creation. Copernicus demoted the earth to a mere, somewhat peripheral, speck in the galaxy. This was, according to Freud, the *cosmic* offense. Then came Darwin. He deprived man of his anthropocentric consciousness. Man, who had been in the center of creation, became a mere chance product, as it were, of an evolutional process which did not seem to possess any transcendental principle. This was the *bio-*

logical offense. Until the time of Freud, men took it for granted that all contents of their consciousness had a tinge of spontaneity and free creativeness. With Freud, however, our conscious experiences became a mere surface ripple over an ocean of unconscious currents which are derived from deep biological strata and exert a powerful determining influence on our thoughts and actions. This was the *psychological* offense. Nobody has ever, with so few words, made a more profound remark on the entire cultural history of the West since the Renaissance. It would not be difficult to demonstrate that the *offense* is not as much due to hurt pride, as Freud implied in his remark, but to the deeply rooted *theandric* consciousness which is a heritage of the West, and which belongs to the very essence of Judaeo-Christian thought. However, to discuss this would lead us too far afield. Freud, incidentally, forgot one other great offender, Karl Marx. For dialectic materialism implies another *beleidigung,* namely, the assumption that all creative values, such as religion, art, and culture, are determined by, and secondary to, the state of material production. This was what one might call the *cultural* offense. It is perhaps no coincidence that, contrary to Copernicus and Darwin, both Freud and Marx provided their philosophical smoke trails themselves. Both had a keen sensitivity to the conventional lies of bourgeois, nineteenth-century civilization, and their tendency to *debunk* was based on motives which were anything but materialistic. Berdyaev has demonstrated the essentially messianic character which underlies the mythology of dialectic materialism. Thomas Mann, on the other hand, pointed out that the principle of sublimation, the "ideal" solution of neurotic conflicts, makes Freud a true humanist. Both Freud and Marx were fed, without being aware of it, by the noblest Jewish cultural tradition.

But it seems to be an intrinsic law governing revolutions that their original pathos is not maintained. It is as if they contained some sort of principle of entropy leading to nihilism. The cultural offense led to Stalinism, the biological offense led, via such people as Gobineau and Nietzsche, to Hitler. Where, then, is the psychological offense going to lead? This, of course, is difficult to foretell in concrete terms. However, it is worth while analyzing the actual present currents. The philosophical smoke trails of modern psychology implies a *reductive* principle. This is again most clear and unequivocal in the Freudian teaching. On the basis of Freud's philosophical writings we might, for instance, say that God is "nothing but" a father image. In fact, Freud says so himself. We might say that Communion is "nothing but" some form of oral eroticism, or cannibalistic father introjection, or something of that sort. This reductive principle could be called the philosophy of "nothing but." What actually happens here is an inversion, an upside-down of Platonism. Just as Marx says proudly that he turned the Hegelian philosophy upside down, Freud, obviously without being aware of it, has done the same thing to Plato. A Platonic philosopher might say: "Even in our attitude to our earthly father we can conceive a crude image of our attitude to God," "Even in the earliest, most primitive cannibalistic rituals we see a foreshadowing of the idea of Communion." However, this presupposes that universal ideas are not something purely accidental to the mind, and that matter can be imbued by spirit. Once we begin to reduce the spiritual to the material we are compelled never to regard man in his entirety but only from one single aspect at a time—either the economic or the biological, or the psychological. This is quite clear in the light of what happened during the last century. It could probably be demonstrated that this approach to the human problem is the only one which makes it possible to *manage* large numbers of people.

However, let us go back to the practical point in question. Those who feel that moral concepts should be re-examined on the basis of objective science are, it seems, chiefly influenced by various motives. For instance, they see patients who are fettered and warped by the fear of eternal damnation, who seem to be hemmed in by some peculiar religious consideration in every step they take. The creativeness of the individual seems to be forever blocked by a sense of guilt. It is true that a false Puritanism and (in the Catholic Church) a strong Jansenistic trend here and there have slain many victims. Most people's concept of morality has become purely negative, and taking the history of some of our patients, we begin to wonder whether Christianity is not for them an intricate system of prohibitions. Even those patients whose neurosis does not choose this particular pattern, when they are asked about the subject of religion, frequently reply: "Oh, as far as religion is concerned, I am all right, I don't . . ." and then there follows an enumeration of all the things they do *not* do. What we need is a tremendous program of re-education of those who are concerned with the teaching of religion.

Many present-day psychiatrists, however, do not see this phenomenon as an accidental one which can be dissociated from the problem of religion without touching upon its essential truths. They feel that the social sciences are under an obligation, with objective and detached methods, to abolish or to reshape those basic concepts themselves rather than their false objectivation. This, however, is a methodological error. All philosophers, from Aristotle to Bergson, from Plato to Whitehead, agree that the world of values is inaccessible to the methods used by the sciences. One of our foremost scientists, Conant, warns us not to try to apply "accumulative knowledge" to problems which are essentially those of "poetry and philosophy." Conant modifies Bacon's threefold division of the realm of learning and speaks of accumulative, poetic and philosophic knowledge. "Whereas the idea of progress," Conant says, "is both valid and significant, in the first category (accumulative knowledge), in the other two the concept is not only invalid but a positive deterrent to relevant undertakings. . . . For it is obvious that poesy or poetry, on the one hand, and philosophy, on the other, together hold the keys to man's immediate future, including the advance of accumulative knowledge. . . ."

The argument implied in Freud's writings on religion, and even more so in numerous publications of comparative psychologists, social psychologists and psychoanalysts, runs approximately as follows: If I examine "religion" with the tools of psychoanalysis and of comparative psychology, the moral and supernatural values lose their absoluteness, and they can be reduced by this method to something which is determined by numerous extraneous and accidental factors. This is the fallacy of scientism of which Conant is obviously aware. Just as there were some scholastic philosophers who erroneously applied philosophical methods to problems pertaining to science, the proponents of scientism succumb to the opposite error. Supposing a man set out to do scientific research on Beethoven's Ninth Symphony. Such a man might go into Beethoven's childhood history, his emotional development, and the social and cultural constellation in Europe of the 1820's. He might then do a study of the physics and mechanics of the various instruments, the average number of vibrations produced at any given time during the performance of the symphony. He might supply these data graphically and with mathematical formulations. All this would mean a laborious task, and a huge compilation of scientific material. But has our research worker "explained" or "understood" one bar of the Ninth Symphony? Of course he has not; there is an essence to this phenomenon which we call Beethoven's Ninth Symphony which the man has not even touched by his objective investigations. It would be preposterous to assume that, on the basis of his results, he might discover errors in the structure of the Ninth Symphony, or correct it.

What holds true with reference to aesthetic values holds equally true with reference to religious and moral ideas. "Accumulative knowledge" does not pertain to them. Now these questions are far from being of a purely academic and abstract nature, because the philosophical superstructure of psychology, as it manifested itself in Freud's writings on religion, and in the works of numerous comparative sociologists, psychoanalysts and anthropologists, reaches far beyond those writings. Its spirit has become an ill-defined, never quite clearly formulated *attitude* of many of those who deal with human beings in the field of psychology, medical psychology and social work.

To disentangle that philosophical superstructure from the factual material of psychological observation is by no means as easy as might be supposed. And once we shall have achieved that task we shall have to integrate this present-day knowledge of man with the Christian idea of man. It is quite true that all factual observations of psychoanalysis are perfectly compatible with religion. However, compatibility, or rather the lack of incompatibility, is not enough. The task of integration is formidable and, as we have indicated above, cannot be isolated from the general problem of the fate of a Christian anthropology in the cultural development of the West since the Renaissance.

If we are to undertake this task we already have a few points in our favor. To begin with, Freud's method is not "scientific" in a mechanistic sense. His ingenious observations were made by intuition and empathy. Jaspers once pointed out that one must not be misled by Freud's terminology. He used words such as "splitting-off," "sublimination," "preservation of libidinal energy," and this practice is due to the fact that he was a typical child of the nineteenth century, originally a scientist himself, in love with science and with the frills of science. However, his method has actually nothing to do with quantification; it is an "understanding" type of psychology, and much more akin to the methods of such psychologists as Shakespeare and Tolstoy than to the thinking of those who hold a mechanistic outlook on man. It is "poetic knowledge" in the sense of Conant and its very method has never been dehumanized.

Moreover, those who believe in the primacy of the spirit are looking at these issues from a vantage point which Freud himself did not have. Had he himself known and recognized a psychology (knowledge of the *psyche*) other than natural, as explored by, let us say, Teresa of Avila, he would not have been shaken in any one of his fundamental discoveries, but his insights would have taken on a third dimension, and he would, with his genius, have built something of a tremendous grandeur. As it is, he has supplied only one blueprint and it is for those who come later to add a few storeys. In this connection it is interesting to read his short and brilliant essay on Dostoevski and *The Brothers Karamazov*. There he gave a penetrating analysis of the psychological background in Dostoevski's own life; he was full of praise of the profound psychology displayed in the novel but he missed entirely the main point—the spiritual drama. He had a blind spot for it. Those among us, however, who "see both sides," are at an advantage when it comes to the task of integration. This implies also a duty. If we do not contribute to this task we are as guilty as those who discovered, much too late, the fact that in the pathos of Karl Marx—in his critical analysis of the capitalist structure of society and of the ills of an industrial civilization—there was an entire world of thoughts which should have been taken up eagerly by Christians and purged of philosophical errors.

Unless we achieve this integration, mankind will be in the position of a patient whom I encountered during my student days. He was a Russian Jew afflicted with a psychosis. Apart from his psychotic symptoms, which I have forgotten, he was deeply religious and talked a good deal about the Messiah. Our teacher in psychiatry was a charming, very cultured professor who belonged to a school of thought in psychiatry which thinks it is able to explain everything in terms of localization in various areas of the brain. After our patient had been presented in conference, the professor called him back once more from the door and said: "Incidentally, that idea about the Messiah, that is nonsense . . . forget about it!"

It seems peculiar that, with the exception of Father White's interesting studies, Jung has received so little attention by Catholic psychologists.

Here is a man who started off on the basis of traditional and academic psychiatry, and came, via psychoanalytical methods, purely clinically, to observations about the human mind, some of which bear startling resemblance to "observations" of the mystics. Such a development is fascinating if we regard it as a symptom of the cultural history of our time. Why, then, do most Catholic psychologists make a wide circle around this phenomenon? There seem to be several reasons for this. Firstly, Jung's observations are much more aphoristic than those of Freud, and do not lend themselves to systematization. Secondly, there is a strong element of gnosis. The Freudian psychology remains strictly on the "natural plane," it is by its very nature agnostic, and therefore not "dangerous." Thirdly, this form of knowledge frequently leads to some sort of noncommittal mysticism, a mysticism without discipline, so that in the end there remains a museum of religious experiences, with Christian, Hindu, Buddhist, etc., collector's items. (There is no true mysticism without ascesis, as Newman said.)

But all this would make it seem even more necessary to study Jung's psychology carefully and separate that which is genuine from that which is purely speculative, even if it were only for the fact that he was the first one to follow the roots of the neurosis to where they transcend the biological layer.

However, to come back to our initial point. It is not right to accept of psychoanalysis only the great factual discoveries and the therapeutic boon. We are forced to look closely at the philosophical superstructure. But the more we have probed the "nature" of man, the more we seem to have stripped him of the supernatural. This is what makes Freud's remark, quoted in the beginning of this article, so uncanny. Copernicus, Darwin, Marx, Freud—what a humiliating dénouement. First we are thrown out of a geocentric cosmos, then out of an anthropocentric life; no wonder that our social achievements arise out of greed, and our ideas are masked impulses. However, if we see that first things come first, if we integrate the tremendous discoveries into a cosmology and into an anthropology in which Grace penetrates Nature, then we shall be enriched instead of impoverished, and we shall feel humbled instead of humiliated.

The Hallowing of All Life

✶

H. A. REINHOLD

REV. H. A. REINHOLD, *a native of Hamburg, Germany, and one of the founders of the Apostolate of the Sea, is now pastor of Saint Joseph's Church, Sunnyside, Washington. He is one of the leaders of the liturgical movement in the United States and author of* The Soul Afire.

✶

THE fall ember days are over: we have thanked God in our churches for the harvest in solemn fasts, hymns and prayers. In austere and beautiful Masses of this autumnal season even the Holy Eucharist has been related to harvest and daily life. With our national holiday of Thanksgiving over a month off, we have time to ponder sufficiently over this friendly intermingling of the natural and supernatural.

And to judge from the index of the *Rituale Romanum* there is no precinct of life on which the Church does not bestow a blessing of some kind. But perhaps it is better first to say what this *Rituale Romanum* is. It is the special book of rites and blessings for the sacraments and sacramentals not contained in the Roman Missal or the office book of the bishop or pontiff, the *Pontificale Romanum*. Its body contains twelve chapters or "titles," a general introduction on baptism, on penance, on the Holy Eucharist, the rites of the sick, the dying and deceased, and matrimony. These sacraments take up about a third of the book, seven titles. The eighth title contains those blessings which occur during the year, like holy water, blessing of the Easter food, the altar apparel and vessels. Title nine contains the many processions of the church calendar and in times of special need. Then follow a collection of approved litanies, exorcisms and rules for parish archives. The appendix, which is almost as voluminous as the body of the book itself, complements the above titles and adds innumerable blessings from church bells to scapulars, from bees to cow stables, from printing presses to medals.

This enumeration, dry as it is, is necessary to show what a wealth of rites and hallowings there are stored up in books of which even more devout Catholics hardly ever hear about or from which they ever see a single word or action. Of course, some blessings are restricted to specific areas, like the great number approved only for the Archdiocese of Cologne, among which there is one for water, bread and salt in honor of Saint Hubert against rabies caused by dog bites. Strange as it sounds to our ears, its text is beautiful and strong, almost conjuring the miracle which before Louis Pasteur was the only thing that could save men from that terrible affliction. Naturally, with miracles you have to take your chances, and if human science has freed mankind from this scourge, Saint Hubert will certainly not mind his blessing being shelved. After all, he is a saint and saints have never opposed anything that helped mankind. There is nothing overconfident or magical in these prayers; they all refer us back to God Almighty and His mercy and kindness. Has not Christ promised miracles to those who believe in Him, like drinking poison without harm and picking up snakes without danger? If our faith were as a mustard seed we would, like Gregory Thaumaturgos, tell a mountain to move and it would obey.

A blessing like Saint Hubert's and similar ones seem to lie on the outer fringe of the liturgical life, even though we realize how they really are centered in the light of faith and the words of the Gospel. But the *Rituale* contains a great many things that are easier to link with those visible signs Christ Himself sanctioned and which since the high Middle Ages have been singled out by theology for the name of sacraments. Sacred words and things like bread, wine, water and oil are the symbols Christ Himself endowed with a new significance that went beyond signification and carried in themselves the greater reality, divine life. There is nothing surprising in this "materialization" as long as the Word Himself became flesh. Of course, materialization is an erroneous term anyway—since neither Christ becomes bread in the Eucharist, nor does the Holy Spirit become oil in the consecration of chrism. In this the slanderers of sacramentalism, who protest in the name of the Spirit, all err. After all, what is material in these sacred signs is only what carries their signification. These fine distinctions are hard to understand it is true, but if you don't want to accept in childlike faith on Christ's word what has been handed down through the living tradition of the Church, you will just have to do what scholasticism did: reason things out to the limit of human understanding. You can't stop half way because things become so involved and subtle that all the theologians' fun of finding something like an equation gets lost over their strain and labor of getting things nicely labeled and stacked in orderly piles. How much more repulsive for one looking for simple truth and life!

A purist might claim that he would be willing to accept those seven sacred signs for which Christ Himself has pledged His divine authority. What the Church has developed further he might not be willing to accept. Non-Catholic scholars like Usener have always suspected that a great deal of the ritual of the Church was picked up from pagan sources and then "baptized." They admire the Church for her clever policy toward the rude and newly converted nations. The Celtic spring solstice fires, which Patrick brought into the Church changing them into the New Fire of the Easter vigil—as one version has the story—is an example of this shrewd pedagogy. Others point to the date of our present Christmas feast, which coincides with the winter solstice and the pagan birthday of the invincible sun. There are dozens of instances where historians have pointed with gloating to what they think a sort of pagan "skeleton in the closet" of Mother Church—things of a disreputable ancestry. It causes them a wicked joy to have found out that Roman Catholicism is, after all, pagan with a thin Christian veneer. The more intelligent ones, like Harnack, just throw up their hands and shake their heads in tolerant surprise. They shrug their shoulders and look with one eye on such sublime mystics as Saint Teresa or Meister Eckhart, and with the other on such gross things as the blessing of beer and cheese, and all they are able to muster in a last effort of charity and justice is a grand word: *complexio oppositorum*. The Church, to them, is an incredibly complex affair of the sublime and the trite. But so is life, so is man! Some will admit that as a good mother she had to stoop to the Polish peasant, the German burgher and the French feudal nobleman as well as the poor illiterates in the Abruzzi backwoods and on Sicilian manorial estates. Has she not only recently permitted Christians in Japan to bow to the symbols of state? Would not China by now be a Christian country if Father Matteo Ricci, S.J., had had it his way, sparing old traditions and folklore which could have easily been baptized?

Perhaps these purists will agree that the Church was a master of compromise and thus a good educator, but they will say that this admixture of mud now has to be melted out of the true gold of Christ's real message. The time of worshiping God in spirit and truth has come. Shall we not now in our scientific and enlightened age drop these things, or at least leave them to Sicily, Ireland, Poland and the Spanish-speaking countries, where people seem to be fond of them? At least, where all these things are unusual, don't let us introduce them. Joseph Andreas Jungmann, in his great book, *The Gospel and Our Way of Evangelizing the World,* actually advises us not to revive those rites which people, as he thinks, fortunately have forgotten. Here is one man within the fold who implicitly accepts the verdict of outsiders that Holy Mother should switch from her former pedagogy of religious and intellectual unions to adult education and should forget the things she did for man when he was in the kindergarten stage of development.

Let us see if this is really what the Church wants us to do and if not, why we could not claim that here in the New World, where we live among an enormous non-Catholic majority, we should be allowed to drop these nonessentials. Unless there are confidential instructions higher up, I have not seen anything in writing which would justify such a policy. It is true, articles have appeared which discourage such things as the Candlemas procession. Reason: it is not now a custom here and its introduction would be a break in our national tradition which is just as good as other countries' local customs. I would diagnose this as a bad case of "legalitis," which means that you can build up a foolproof argument, if you stick to the words of your law book, but that you forget history and the great setting out of which you have taken your case. Historically, for instance, this Candlemas procession, which is one of the sacramentals, could simply not be carried out when the Church here was a missionary institution, poor, understaffed, hemmed in by prejudice. But now that the others have become accustomed to flowing purple robes, lavish churches, beautiful convents and magnificent Catholic campuses, could we not with even better reason afford to begin to celebrate the entire liturgy as it is on the books? Voluntary poverty certainly helps the spreading of the Gospel, but liturgical destitution and parsimony is hardly the thing the poor demand of Christ's Church.

Yet churchings, blessing of houses, of the bridal chamber, of pilgrims, of the little ones, of food and harvest, of wine and beer, of the expectant mother and of the sick are certainly the exception in our days. Aren't they all a warm breath from the loving heart of our mother? Granted they are not sacraments working through a consecration, or as theology terms it, *ex opere operato*. They do not transsubstantiate things. But they do take things out of the ordinary, secular world and put them to the service of God. They flow from the seven Sacraments as an ever-broadening river receives its life from the clear and live mountain stream at its head. If matrimony is a sacrament, what is more natural than to bless the house, the bridal chamber, the expectant mother? Should her first visit in church not be a triumphant entry with candle light and song of psalms, Christ meeting her at the gate in the person of his priest? What a tribute to motherhood, what a lighting up of nature to a new vision! Is it so strange that the Church should imitate Christ and call her infants to the altar or the knees of the visiting priest for a special blessing? Instead of having to pat Pat on the back and pull Joan's pigtails in a teasing way or making just a stiff social call, I have always felt I wish the people would get over our mutual embarrassment during house visits by just asking me to do what priests do best: blessing.

The same seems to be true about the sick. They will go and tell you all about their last injection and where it aches and pains; old people will even insist on showing you their wounds and scars, all in a very nice, unself-conscious and trusting way; but if you could read them a part of the beautiful service of the *Visitation of the Sick,* Gospel and all, I suppose they would feel better and holier and not just see in you a nice chap who dropped in out of pure human kindness (which I certainly do not want to belittle or discourage). Is not that what our people really expect, even if they like to see Father unbend and tell a good joke or listen patiently to woes and tears? One can bring a whiff from the sanctuary without leaving an oil slick behind.

Looking at these blessings, it becomes evident that some of them are simply elaborations of the sacraments, e.g., the four minor orders leading up to the priesthood. Holy water is derived from the idea of baptism, or the blessing of wine on the feast of Saint John the Evangelist and of bread on Saint Agatha's feast relate us to the Eucharist. Other connections have been pointed out before. Some, any of the faithful may draw. But it is not evident for everybody that the well-known grace before meals is especially timely when it is sung in religious communities, as it is called, "eucharistic" in spirit, thus linking the family meal in each house to the family meal at the altar. Its Our Father, its versicles taken from the old eucharistic Psalm 33, and its blessing make it almost visibly an "agape," a meal of love related to the Mass. Nobody is unimpressed by the monastic custom of chanting these prayers and then partaking of food of the body, while a reader offers food to the mind.

If we still carried out these lovable rites which seem to take all secular vulgarity out of the simplest human things and give value and significance to the most trite of them, certainly our understanding of the real sacraments would be more profound. We would not have to fear that in our sacramental lives we were escaping "reality" and lived in a fairy world of escapist illusions. Those things are so truly realistic. The kingdom of God here really rubs elbows with the humble and ordinary things that make up the life even of the chosen people of God. If we did all we could do there would be a tremendous change of attitude. The incorporation of our whole lives into the divine sacrifice could be grasped with our naked hands and the slowest-witted child could see such obvious relations.

What makes a priest regret that most sacramentals have lapsed from practice and memory is not only that it is now so much more difficult to let the people completely see the significance of the sacramental world, as a world, an organism full of meaning, related to life and its stages, with proportion and perspective and not just disconnected devices to fool the devil and hell, but another observation which brings to mind equally serious consideration. The strange fact is that some sacramentals did survive and are very much sought after. As a matter of fact, they are extremely popular: the protective ones, the safety devices—I mean certain medals and blessings. If we try to arrange the sacramentals in concentric circles around the seven sacraments according to their nearness and relationship to them, to salvation, to worship of God and sacrifice, to the "consecration of the world" initiated in Christ's incarnation, then these things are certainly where the planet Neptune is in the solar circle: on the outer fringe of the economy of salvation. Their immense popularity does not have to be discouraged, because some overconscientious men may see dangerous inclination toward superstition in them. The average Catholic knows, at least in theory, the difference between a Saint Christopher's medal and a rabbit's foot, a blessed object and a charm or amulet. Of course, non-Catholics often wonder, if this theoretical knowledge is not nullified through its practical application. But I think that nobody need start a campaign of purification of pagan remnants in people's minds, if the things closer to the center, more significant, more centered on God are duly emphasized, if we become conscious of degrees, of perspective, of differing qualities, of interrelationships. The kingdom of heaven comes to the whole man, and if Christ allows us to ask for bread and tells us that every hair on our head is counted, we may safely express our faith in God's all-embracing providence by hanging a medal on our child's or departing soldier's neck. However, it is a time, when isolated from and not complemented by a whole world of sacred elevation of little things and small events, those things indeed look void of real sacred significance.

You can take two attitudes: one would be to be sparse with material signs in the religious sphere. Prune down to their utmost minimum those old sacramentals which to purists seem to have a stark medieval flavor. Let us stick to what the Church guarantees: the seven sacraments and all that is necessary to perform them. That would be a sort of Catholic puritanism. But our puritans and utilitarians ought to be consistent. If the Candlemas procession and churching is no good, then the miraculous medal and blessing of throats is no better; none of them was introduced by the Lord, and while the first two are divine worship with God as the center, the latter are centered around something less important, the human ego, at least comparatively. You don't want to do that? Then let us be consistent. Bring back all of the missing links.

Art and Matter

DAVID ROSS KING

REV. DAVID ROSS KING, *who holds degrees from St. John's University, Collegeville, Minn., Laval University of Quebec and the University of Toronto, is diocesan superintendent of schools in Superior, Wisconsin.*

SINCE, as Scripture and Fathers teach, all things are made for God's glory, a test of man's religion in this material world is his use of things material: this is an index to our Catholicism.

In the mystery of the incarnation we find the perfect example of the use of matter: the human nature of Jesus, with its essential material constituent, was an instrument, the instrument conjoined to his divinity for glorification and sanctification. In Him was elevated all material creation with the immaterial; all things in Him are lifted up. Thus the world, made in the beginning as a paean to the godhead, is restored to its first purpose.

Man's use of matter, of creation, is a way of carrying on the work of redemption, a work that will be complete only at the end of time when all things will have been restored to God in Christ. In this work of elevating creation the role of the Church is supreme. She is more than our leader, our teacher. She is herself the perfect exemplification of the employment of things material to a supernatural end: she is *the great sacrament*. She uses, moreover, material realities as divinely conceived and effected and effective instruments of salvation, and these, applied to the bodies of men, accomplish human elevation. The Church, Christianity, is essentially sacramental.

Saint Paul exclaimed: "Great is the mystery *(sacramentum)* of piety: who was manifested in the flesh, justified in spirit, seen by angels, was preached among the nations, believed on in the world, taken up in glory."

If the historical Christ was thus a sacrament, the Church too, the very continuation of the incarnation into space and time, is a sacrament. So also ought each member of the mystical Christ become in life and works: a sign and symbol and channel of grace that will cause men and things to return to their head, which is Christ, and a sign and symbol and epiphany of supernatural realities.

In his mystical life in the Church Christ still lives among men in earthly guise and communicates his life to us by transfigured earthly means, that assuming to himself our earthliness he may make us partakers of his divinity.

Thus the sacramental Church reverences and makes holy use of those elements divinely chosen as effective signs: the water of regeneration, the oil of healing and consecration, the bread and wine of sacrifice and nourishment. Hers is necessarily, then, a sacramental view of the whole universe. Avoiding the crudities of pantheism and the old "return to God," she recognizes whatsoever she finds in nature as manifestations of God's power and beauty and goodness, and she seeks to rededicate all matter to its maker by sacraments and sacramental blessings: she strives to free the material universe of diabolical bonds so that again it may untrammeled praise its Lord.

I remember how, when very young, I was troubled to find the song of the three youths assigned in the missal to thanksgiving after Mass. What had fish and frosts and fountains to do with thanksgiving after Communion (that is what it then was, I fear, rather than thanksgiving after Mass)? A great deal, I was to learn. When can brute nature, made for praise, better express itself than when he who has physically fed on its Lord and harbors Him safe lifts his voice in thanks.

All ye works of the Lord, bless the Lord:
praise and exalt Him above all forever. . . .

The postcommunion of the Sunday within the octave of Ascension says that we ought *always,* after Communion, remain in the very act of giving thanks; *ut in gratiarum semper actione maneamus.* Besides our own virtuous life, is there another lasting thanksgiving: the praise of creation itself, to which briefly we give voice on its behalf, that afterwards it may go on thanking on our behalf?

In all our life's work we are to make fuller creation's praise of God, lending it our intelligence, giving it place in our reasonable service of the Lord, as often as we make proper use of material elements. Otherwise, our "creative work" becomes desecration, rather than creation.

No one has expressed better than Gerard Manley Hopkins the universality of the Christian's praise:

> You do say grace at meals and thank and praise God for your daily bread, so far so good, but thank and praise Him now for everything. When a man is in God's grace and free from mortal sin, then everything that he does, so long as there is no sin in it, gives God glory and what does not give Him glory has some, however little, sin in it. It is not only prayer that gives God glory, but work. Smiting on an anvil, sawing a beam, whitewashing a wall, driving horses, sweeping, scouring, everything gives God some glory if being in His grace you do it as your duty. To go to communion worthily gives God great glory, but to take food in thankfulness and temperance gives Him glory too. To lift up the hands in prayer gives God glory, but a man with a dungfork in his hand, a woman with a sloppail, give Him glory too. He is so great that all things give Him glory if you mean they should. So then, my brethren, live.

Satan perverts this order, "wreathing nature and as it were constricting it to his purposes." So does man when he uses things material meanly, selfishly or as ends. So also does man when he rejects the material world contemptuously as injurious to what he regards as his soul's purity, when he tries to live as though he were of the angelic order: this is the subtler, more insidious error.

The Church is a mystery: water and spirit, blood and spirit, flesh and spirit. Life in the Church demands of her members wholeness, harmonious employment of body and spirit, of water and wine, of bread and oil.

Years ago I took down a saying whose author's name (one of the Fathers, I believe) has left me: "This is the hidden and despicable poison of your heresy, that you represent the grace of Christ as His example, not His gift, alleging that man is justified by imitating Him, not by the ministration of the holy Spirit." This heresy is apparent in much of modern devotion and consequently in the lives of Christians: Christianity is become for many a mere ethical imitation of Christ, a "following" of Christ. To more anciently traditional Catholic thought it is more: it is a transforming elevation, *by God Himself,* of man, with all he makes use of holily, to a new plane of being. To the baptized is given the Midas touch.

The world was made for God's glory. This is a truth and a principle: on it man can base fruitful living. A positive attitude towards the world of God's making and the devil's and man's corrupting will help restore God's own *(sui et suae et sua)* to him. As Father Hopkins so happily said, all things are "charged with love, are charged with God and if we know how to touch them give off sparks and take fire, yield drops and flow, ring and tell of Him."

Departmentalization of the Christian's life has been one of the tragic results of the failure to *acknowledge* God's world, and has given a sterile, unreal, blasé, Sunday Christianity to times that perish for want of fruitful, real, mystical, daily Christianity. Men today too, as when Jesus *walked* the earth (not disdaining its surface) on feet (so real) and had not whereon to lay His head (so real! needing most really a resting place, material and comforting), have eyes and ears, worn hands; to those too come the invitations: "Taste and see, take and eat, come and be comforted."

Hence need of Christian art, as well as the sacraments of Christ. "Need?" one may ask. Have not men made pictures and statues these many centuries (and faster and cheaper than ever in this mechanized age), and are not the churches and our homes filled with them? Yes. But are these always representations that are sanctified and that sanctify? Have they the "sacramental character"?

In much religious art have we not found "the immensities of religion, of humanity's needs and humanity's destiny, set aside, and in their place," to quote Father Gerald Vann, "only the thoughts that sooth and lull the individual—a lace-edged, flower-strewn covering over the mouth of hell"? Is not this great Dominican correct in charging, moreover, that we favor, over the idea of making, a purely passive, self-indulgent receptivity?

There are those who like to believe that all art must preach some explicit message, thrust forward some pious sentiment, illustrate a text: this is the manner of both the appleblossom Madonnas and the ads for perfume and nail lacquer ("Red Apple," "Bachelor's Carnation," "Escape in the Night") with whose purposes and technique those of the former may be identified. But art speaks in symbol, uses symbol to make us aware of reality, not of illusion: it draws *aside* the veil. I can be as aware of God, of the holiness of his works, before a still life as before a crucifixion, perhaps more so.

I believe that Julian Green did the art of Catholics in America a service when he faced honestly "the awful spell cast over religious sensibility by the great man whom our fathers called Sanzio." Raphael did indeed "saturate and infect the minds of millions with dull commonplaces about the gospel . . . crowding the invisible with chromos." How right is Mr. Green: "Raphael is probably one of the most dangerous heretics since the Church began; his heresy is a subtle one which begins with a yawn and ends with nausea. His good intentions are as plentiful as they are demoralizing. He kills devotion with an almost infallible aim. Charity turns into a lump of ice under his nefarious gaze, and great though he was, the fact that he ever touched a paintbrush is the equivalent of one of those spiritual disasters from which the world has apparently not recovered."

We have not recovered. Eric Gill wrote of such artists: "What things *are* does not interest them: they are only concerned with how things look. And this idea pervades the whole world. So that even believers are corrupted by it." What exactly have been the effects of this corruptive "classic" influence upon the art of our churches and homes? Upon the people? Has not art without the truly Christian character tended to form people without Christian character? The nadir of the tragedy, I am persuaded, is in the negation of reverence. Before the images the beholder feels either comfortably patronizing or cozily chummy; he may experience something akin to calf love; but he doesn't fall irresistibly to his knees. Who could feel before the Madonna della Sedia his own littleness and his own dignity, the majesty of the divine, the splendor of God's holy works, as he might before the mosaics of San Vitale in Ravenna or the tympanum of Moissac or a "Head of Christ" by Rouault? The art which has been spawned on false classicism by geniuses themselves misbegotten of imperfect Catholicism has sought escape from reality rather than awesome penetration into reality, just as have those allegedly devotional books that drool gluttonously over a sugar candy heaven and shudder daintily before the spectacle of God's material creation, belittling the body, for example, as the prison-house of the spirit from which on death's blessed day the soul will at length escape, like a bird from its hated cage (in all this, what of the resurrection of the blessed body, what of the most holy resurrection of the Son of Man, wherein is contained mystically the ennoblement of all our visible universe?).

Our creation, art, already an honoring of God if purely and humbly done, must be employed in His service, His praise, not our own; art's vocation is to elevate the whole man, body and spirit, for God's sake, rather than to glamorize self-indulgence for the flesh's sake.

Yet for reverence, sacred and essential to a true Christian spirit, reverence for God and all the works of God, has been substituted sentiment, and for love has been substituted sensuality. Look at our "Christs at the Helm," our St. Bernadettes (heavy with lip rouge and dreamy-eyed with false lashes)—here is love as believed in and hoped for and parodied by the world of which Satan is prince and sly master. In such works of art, common and commercial, big-selling and properly approved, I find no trace of divine love or of its elevation of all things unto itself. And here is the irony: the "spirituals" in negating the excellence of matter produce the most fleshly art, sweet with the sweetness of forbidden fruit. It is art that ministers to man for man's sake instead of ministering to man for God's sake.

Such art, however many its good intentions and sacred subjects, advances the standard of Satan, "the thrower of things off the track . . . (who) brought in the law of decay and consumption in inanimate nature, death in the vegetable and animal world, moral death and original sin in the world of man," who tried "to possess himself of the sovereignty of things," Satan whose song Gerard Manley Hopkins speaks of as "a dwelling on his own beauty, an instressing of his own inscape, and like a performance on the organ and instrument of his own being," which aboriginal hymn in his own praise "became an incantation: others were drawn in; it became a concert of voices, a concerting of self-praise, an enchantment, a magic, by which they were dizzied, dazzled, and bewitched."

The true artist, the maker, is called to help restore the fallen world, the stolen world; to restore man's dominion over matter, granted first to Adam who called the beasts by their names and they obeyed him, the dominion given man for God's sake and appropriated by Satan for his own purposes. Thus Church and artist have a single aim: to glorify God by giving Him back the praise of His creation intelligently, holily employed. And the artist is actively engaged, as should also those be who behold his work, in the religious use of matter; he is not to tie himself and his spectators to so much matter for self-indulgence (to be dizzied, dazzled, bewitched), rather both are to be elevated into conscious divine praise by what is done and seen. This is holy work, holy in its doing and in its effects.

In the family, cell of Church and society, art can most effectively fulfill its role as an instrument of sanctification. There especially will its "sacramental character" become evident. In the home the young behold and hear, they are taught to make. Always it is the vocation of parents, in every aspect of life (recognized and taught as integral, supernaturalized life—not departmentalized life), to raise up children in reverence and in love of God and His creatures, in reverent and loving employment of whatever good gifts come from the Giver of good and perfect gifts, the Father of lights Who enlightens through His *incarnate* Son Who appeared in this world as the great sacrament, the great visible sanctifying sign. If a child be not taught to make well, lovingly, reverently, at home, how shall he be fully Christian? For all his life he will make, he will employ things material. And this is art: to make well, whether the simplest objects or the most sublime.

But if parents are to teach a child to make well, to reverence matter, to lift it up in God's praise rather than to be dragged down by it, they must surround him, perceptive as he is, with good art. Here is the opportunity and the responsibility of artists and teachers: to supply what is needed. If I have spoken with little approval of those corruptive, earthly, enervating masterpieces of renaissance and postrenaissance techniques (so aptly called by James Joyce "masterplasters," as we know them in commercial reproduction), I should nevertheless point out that they are, undeniably, intelligible. Intelligible to the oft-mentioned man in the street, to the wife and children in the home. If they go to the heart of the wrong way (for as Father Jungmann, the distinguished Jesuit philosopher, so aptly says, citing the Raphael Madonnas, "the purely natural relations predominate while those of an ecclesiastical-religious nature have faded") at least they do go there, and they do deeply impress the mind and affect the soul if not beyond the natural level. They do not leave beholders of good will perplexed and frightened and unhappy. *Claritas* still counts.

It would be presumptuous to assign a single cause to the ills of Catholicism in our day. Faith is weak in many hearts, we hear; there are many Sunday Catholics, many who are merely fair-weather-this-Sunday-morning Catholics. One cause, surely, is discovered in the representations of sacred persons and themes in the art of our churches and homes. Well might a man grow weak in faith and careless in practice who has been reared among spineless Madonnas, saccharine Sacred Hearts, swivel-hipped St. Josephs, and gaudily garbed Infants of Prague ("genuine crystal eyes, very lifelike, twelve dollars extra"). The yawn begins in childhood and the nausea comes in due time.

If good people survive, lively of faith, in homes bedecked with these vulgar insults to the divine, that only proves anew how limitless is God's mercy and how mighty the power of His grace. He is the great hurdler of obstacles, but that does not justify our placing them. And besides the simple, unquestioning, unruffled, holy Breton peasant (or American citizen) there are men and women of inquiring mind and alert sensibilities: these too have souls to save, they need the ministrations of true, religious art.

Our use of matter is an index to our Catholicism. The artist, aware of the sacramentality of the universe and of life, can become the apostle of an age that needs him. And I do believe that the home will be his special mission field, since the churches are so often, like Tibet and Nepal, closed to him. Since from the homes comes the new generation, in which we place our hopes (as did our fathers unhappily in us), he can plan and influence the future. Just now, please, let him, in honesty and with love, supply what is needed: pictures and statues and objects of devotion plentiful enough and cheap enough and good enough and simple enough to reach fathers and mothers and children. They will bless him. And the wood he uses, and the stone and metal and leather and oil, will, through him, bless and glorify the Lord, their first fashioner.

From the Eternal City

MICHAEL WILLIAMS

MICHAEL WILLIAMS, *founder of* The Commonweal *and its first editor (until 1938) is the author of* The High Romance, Catholicism and the Modern Mind, The Shadow of the Pope *and* The Catholic Church in Action.

WHEN I wrote my last dispatch for *The Commonweal,* I tapped at my typewriter on the steamship *Rex,* bearing two American cardinals to Rome, to exercise their franchise as chief citizens in the City of God by voting for the new Pope. The voyage still holds me in a lingering enchantment, complicated by the strong wizardry that is in the very air of Rome. And before this spell fades away, I must jot down something of the flavor, if not the full force, of the adventure of entering again, after years of absence, into this Roman atmosphere—surcharged with such powerful impressions: opening such tremendous vistas into the past; throbbing with such dynamic forces of the present time; and suggesting, at least, the possibility of magic casements opening on the perilous paths of future time, and the people of tomorrow.

Within this great central city of the ancient, the present, and the developing story of mankind, there is another city that is not of this world, in its spirit and its interests, but which stands within its walls, like a fortress and gateway, guarding yet giving entrance (when passports are in order) to the invisible and the eternal. The ancient town on the Tiber faces and surrounds the town of Peter the Fisher of Souls, with Michael the Archangel of the uplifted sword standing watch and ward by the bridge that joins and also divides town from town. All races and tribes and nations of humanity appear to pass through the streets and courts and halls and shops and market places and churches of both the city of this world and the walled, interior city. And all these people, and their kind by the billions who dwell elsewhere, are really one great family, united in brotherhood, in spite of all differences of language, and color, and type, and class, and garb, and interests and traditions and ideas. No matter what they themselves may think they are doing, or want to do, here or elsewhere, their real business (though most of them do not realize it) is not the work, or the play, or the gossiping, or the quarreling, or any other of their multitudinous affairs—except, of course, as all such affairs play a part in helping or hindering them in the real business of their otherwise incomprehensible lives and doings. This is, namely, to journey through the cities (or the deserts) of this world, to and through the city not of this world, though visibly apparent in it, to reach the world without end; there the life that merely begins in time and space on earth finds its true and permanent purpose.

In Rome, time and eternity are singularly mixed. Today, for instance, is February 23, in the Year of Our Lord 1939. But in the calendar which marks time according to rules related to eternity, for those who live by or follow the way of life established and maintained by the City of the Spirit on Vatican Hill, today is the second day of Lent, in the calendar of the Ecclesiastical Year, and also the Feast of Saint Peter Damien, Bishop, Confessor and Doctor, of the monks of Camboldoli—great reformer of the Church under Pope Saint Leo IX. So in order to get started properly at my set task of writing for the daily papers concerning the great business of the new Pope's election—and what it may mean to mankind, in the Pope's own city, and in the cities of the world—I got up very early and went to Mass. This would help me to get rid of my shipboard hangover of emotions, and build a defense against the bewitching but time-wasting street scenes of Rome and Vatican City: *contadini* coming into town at dawn with wine and fruit and vegetables;

monks and friars and priests and prelates, strolling together, or with soldiers and citizens, through streets ablaze with great masses of spring flowers and odorous with their spices of the earth and the water and the sun; many waters springing night and day from a thousand fountains; churches, palaces and barracks, Egyptian obelisks towering out of ancient mystery over newsstands impudent with flimsy newspapers of today's daily news and gossip.

On the steps of the Carmelite church, across the way from an all-night dram and coffee and tobacco shop, haunted by a few blousy taxi men and hotel porters starting the day, four or five men and women were waiting for the church door to open. As it did so, we all pushed by the heavy leather curtain into the darkness dotted by a few altar candles and lights before the shrines of the two Teresas, John of the Cross and the Mother of God, and the high altar of the Sacrament that unites God with man, and eternity with the processes of time. There was just light enough to read the more essential parts of the prayers for the day, and the unchanging Canon. Remembering that in passing out of fantasy into the reality of things, the job ahead of me was concerned with writing about the Pope who died two weeks ago and the unknown man who is to be our Pope, I found the words of the Introit singularly appropriate. "In the midst of the Church the Lord opened his mouth: and filled him with the spirit of wisdom and understanding"; and, in the Gospel: "You are the light of the world. A city seated on a mountain cannot be hid. Neither do men light a candle and put it under a bushel, but upon a candle stick, that it may shine to all that are in the house; so let your light shine before men that they may see your good works, and glorify your Father Who is in heaven." Surely, Pope Pius opened his mouth in the midst of the Church, speaking both to the Church and the world, in words full of the spirit of wisdom and understanding; surely, too, his successor-to-be will be the light of the world, in a city seated on a mountain, shining before all men.

But . . . but, did the world, or very many within the Church, heed the words of Pius? Will men of the world, or most men and women of the Church, heed and follow the new light soon to be set before them?

The Trappists Go to Utah

THOMAS MERTON

THOMAS MERTON, *author of* The Seven Storey Mountain *and* Seeds of Contemplation, *is a member of the Order of Cistercians of the Strict Observance (Trappists) at the Abbey of Our Lady of Gethsemani in Kentucky.*

WHEN the citizens of St. Louis went to breakfast on the seventh of July, this year [1947], they found strange headlines. In the middle of the usual floods and politics and acts of violence was an item that might almost have concerned ambassadors from Mars. It must have made many good people uneasy to read the startling words: *"Monks in locked car in Station Yards."* Pursuing the subject further, they discovered that the monks in question were the silent Trappists. (In secular newspapers Trappists always end up by being saddled with a "vow of silence.") The car had been there for some hours, and the monks were inside with the blinds down, and many curious people were on the outside in the hot sun, and one porter and three yard detectives were keeping the people on the outside from getting at the monks on the inside. Either that, or they were keeping the monks in the car from escaping. No one could be quite sure which. But in any case, the upshot of the whole affair was that the men inside that railway car were saying Mass.

That is more or less the way it is every time the Cistercians of the Strict Observance—which is their true name—get into the headlines. Newspapermen can never seem to figure them out, and with all their good will they invariably end up by printing something that makes the monks look like the most solemn idiots you ever imagined.

The truth about the men in that railway car is that they were very holy and very simple and very happy and very human men who were going calmly about a piece of work that had been assigned to them by obedience. Perhaps it may help a little to put some flesh and bones on the poor ghosts, and tell people what they were really doing.

There were thirty-five of them. Thirty-four were Trappist monks, brothers and novices from Gethsemani, Kentucky. The thirty-fifth was their Reverend Father Abbot, Dom Mary Frederic Dunne—the first native-born American who managed to survive the austerity of Cistercian life at Gethsemani, where he entered in 1894. He was taking this group of men to Huntsville, Utah, to make Gethsemani's second foundation in three years.

There is a story in that, too. In recent years, especially since the war, the growth of this ancient abbey (which celebrates its centenary next year) has been phenomenal. It is nothing unusual to see ex-servicemen lining up four and five at a time in the chapter room to exchange an "old man" of khaki for the white cloak of a choir novice or the brown cape of a brother. There has hardly been anywhere for them to sleep. Cubicles have been fixed up for them in every odd corner—and still they keep coming. Two world wars have taught America something about the value of asceticism, prayer, penance: and grace has given the young men of our nation something of a thirst for the knowledge of God that is to be had only by those who love Him and give themselves to Him alone.

Of the thirty-four Utah colonists, more than half were Trappists of less than six years' standing, many of these being war veterans. Consequently it was a young and enthusiastic group that crowded that railway car, kneeling in the aisles while one monk held the *mensa* of a portable altar resting on two seats, and another held the chalice steady, and others took turns to offer the Sacrifice of Christ's Body and Blood in the yards of St. Louis's Union Station.

Every moment of the three days' journey was assigned, as far as possible, to some function prescribed in the Cistercian Usages. The monks recited the Canonical Office and the Little Office of the Blessed Virgin. They made their meditations and read the books they had brought with them. (One of their favorites, these days, is "The Spiritual Doctrine of Elizabeth of the Trinity.") They held their daily chapter with the martyrology and all, even the Father Abbot's explanation of the Rule. The only thing omitted was the chapter of faults. The monks got up later than usual, remaining in their berths until 4:30 A.M.—but the reason for this was that they went to bed later at night. No sleeping was allowed outside the regular time, and the rule of silence was kept strictly as usual.

Of course, Cistercian silence is conditional. The Superior can always give permission to speak. But permission is not given at random, even on a train journey. At one point in the trip several of the monks were gathered around their Father Abbot, who had a map of the country they were going through, and they were discussing the landscape. One of the priests—a voluble little man from whom the rule of silence demands considerable self-control—was trying to inveigle permission to tell a funny story. He was consistently rebuffed. Finally he said meekly, but insistently: "Reverend Father, may I say something that has practical value?"

"Yes," said his Abbot, "go away and say three Our Fathers."

The newspaper statement that the Cistercian monks traveled three-quarters of the way across the continent "unseen and unseeing" with the blinds down all the way to Utah was too picturesque to be true. Trappists are, among other things, farmers. And they took a considerable interest in the corn that was growing in Missouri and the wheat that was being harvested in Kansas. But they are, above all, contemplatives: and the Rocky Mountains are nothing to be despised! They have something very eloquent to say about the God Whose power they reflect: and if Trappists did not have an ear to catch that message—who would there be to hear it?

The site of the new monastery is one of the most perfect settings for the contemplative life in the world. The monks have purchased a 1,640-acre ranch at the head of the Ogden Valley, and eighteen miles east of Ogden. It is reached by road through a long canyon carved out of the rock by the Ogden River. At some two thousand feet above Ogden itself, the valley broadens out and the Cistercians have settled in a mile-wide bowl among hills covered with sagebrush and ringed by high mountains which are several miles further away.

When they arrived from Kentucky with its July heat and saw snow-covered Mount Ogden and Ben Lomond the monks began to realize that they had done some traveling! Of course, the summer sun can burn in Utah too, but it is a dry heat, and reports come in from the new monastery that work in the mountains is not unpleasant even when the temperature is high. Damp clothes dry out even before you change them. The contrast with Kentucky is striking. Here dry clothes get wet before you have had them on a minute.

The monks have settled in a wild, lonely spot. To the east of them is nothing but a wilderness without roads or farms. It is a paradise for hunters who, in the past, made the monks' ranch their base, and worked eastward from there. Deer come down to drink at one of the two plentiful springs on the Trappists' ranch, and about the only sound you hear in the valley is the howling of coyotes on the mountainside. At least, that was all you heard until the Cistercians set up their bell and began to ring it for Office and Mass.

It is something new indeed for the Rocky Mountains for a chapel bell to be heard calling monks to choir at two o'clock in the morning, and later ring the consecration of a conventual Mass. And it was not without a certain exultation that the Cistercians bowed to the floor as the Body of Christ was raised above the altar for the first time in that lonely valley! For thousands of years those silent, arid rocks, magnificent in their stark beauty, have nevertheless been waiting for the coming of someone like these Trappists to make them complete. Contemplatives are chosen by God to be the voice of His whole creation, praising him and adoring Him for the inanimate and brute beings that cannot praise him, as well as for those who have reason but will not adore Him, or cannot find the time.

However, it must not be imagined that the Cistercians came to their new home and fell on their knees and remained in prayer for the rest of the week. When a monastery is founded things never seem to be that simple.

There were no dwellings on the property, but a contract had been made for six sections of war-service barracks that had been in use housing German and Italian prisoners during the war. These were to have been hauled to the ranch and set up and made ready in time for the arrival of the Trappists. Unfortunately, when they set foot on the soil of their new home in the early afternoon of July 10 the monks found only a part of the accommodations they had contracted for, and that part was cluttered with lumber and other materials. They cleared a way for themselves and Mass was said and they all broke their fast at about four in the afternoon, except for the Cellarer who was down in Ogden supervising the baggage that was still waiting to be picked up at the station. He came home at 6:00 P.M., hoping for Communion, but he had been forgotten in the confusion.

For the next few days the Trappists slept on the floor or on the predellas of altars in the barrack that was at once chapel, chapter room, refectory and dormitory, cloister, cellar, storeroom and workshop. The secular workmen who were supposed to be hauling the barracks to the site and helping the Trappists to get installed kept going off to do more lucrative jobs, and when the centenary of Brigham Young's arrival in Utah was celebrated barely two weeks after the Trappists came on the scene, the workmen made a long week end of it, but the monks were not sorry as they got a chance to have the Blessed Sacrament reserved during that time.

It was more than two weeks before everything was in order and it was possible to begin leading the regular life in its entirety, singing the office at the proper times and so on. But even now, and for many months and even years to come, manual labor will absorb much more of the monks' day than is usually prescribed.

There is a tremendous amount of work to be done before the new monastery of Our Lady of the Most Holy Trinity becomes a complete and self-sufficing Cistercian unit. The only thing the monks have is a ranch that grows plenty of hay and wheat. For the rest they must build an entire farm and monastery from the ground up. There is, above all, the problem of water. Utah is the land of "dry-farming" and irrigation. The best spring on the monks' land is plentiful indeed but it is a long distance from the good building sites and unless attempts to drill for a spring nearer at hand meet with success, the monks will be faced with the labor and expense of a mile-long pipeline. At present they walk the distance carrying milk cans every day. Several large reservoirs will have to be built, including tanks to catch and store the melting snow in spring.

In Utah, every drop of water is worth money, and the monastery also possesses a handful of "water-right shares" which give it a claim on the organized and rationed supply.

The first question to be settled is that of a real home. The monks do not intend to spend the winter in their army huts if they can avoid it. A temporary monastery is already under construction. It will be made of metal "quonset huts," but will be one of the most elaborate "quonset" structures that has ever been attempted. It will contain everything that belongs to a Cistercian monastery, including Church and cloister and all the "regular" places as well as a guest house for visitors and retreatants. The two-story quadrangular building, centered upon a cloister garth or *préau,* will be spacious and solid since the monks may have to call it their home for twenty or twenty-five years to come.

A site for a permanent monastery has been tentatively chosen on a hilltop which commands a vast view of the valley and the mountains. Just as important as the temporary monastery will be the erection of barns and farm buildings and the formation of a herd of dairy cattle which will be the monastery's chief source of income. The monks will be manufacturing their famous "Port du Salut" cheese. Then there will have to be a garden and orchard, although it is improbable that they will attempt a vineyard. The land itself is extremely rich and promising. Digging the foundations of the temporary monastery they often went through ten or twelve feet of topsoil. A little irrigation will give them splendid crops of potatoes, beets, celery and all the staples of the Cistercian vegetarian diet.

The long Utah winters will present a problem; since there will be no trees to fell and no wood to chop the monks will have to find some indoor work to keep them busy when the snow lies deep on their valley. And it does lie deep, there, too. Last winter there were some two hundred inches of it, and beyond the hills, where there was twice that much, a skiing championship was held.

The Trappists have had a little difficulty in getting acclimatized. The journey and the revolution in their regime upset many stomachs and one of the Fathers had to go to the Benedictine nuns' hospital in Ogden with ulcers, which chose this inappropriate time to declare their presence. Many of the others kept getting violent nosebleeds for the first few days, until they got used to the high altitude.

To compensate for these little trials they have had many consolations, the best of which was the ardent enthusiasm with which they were received not only by the Catholics—who are very much of a minority in Utah—but by non-Catholics as well. Bishop Duane Hunt of Salt Lake City worked hard to persuade Dom Frederic Dunne to make a foundation so far from home and under such numerous handicaps. The coming of the Cistercians is an answer to many fervent pleas and prayers, and consequently the Utah Catholics are delighted to see them. In fact, the Bishop spent the day at the monastery soon after the monks were installed and told them that they were his "only hope." His diocese is one of the largest in the United States and yet it barely occupies two pages in the Catholic Directory. Only half a dozen religious congregations and Orders are represented there by a mission or two and one or two schools and hospitals. Nevertheless the Church is gradually growing in Utah, which is 75 per cent Mormon and in which all the Protestant sects have lost ground consistently since their establishment.

How do the Mormons themselves feel about the Trappists? Individuals have proved themselves very courteous and friendly and no doubt the Cistercians will win the sincere admiration of many in Utah as they have everywhere else. However, it is not likely that the Church of Jesus Christ of the Latter Day Saints will come out with an official public pronouncement welcoming the Trappists with open arms. Incidentally, when the monks packed up their personal belongings for the trip they seem to have found nothing available except cardboard boxes and containers which had previously served to ship whisky and which were obtained from neighboring stores in Kentucky. If the Mormons were paying close attention to the monks as they detrained in Ogden, they must have been very scandalized to see so many boxes labeled "Schenley's" and "Green River." Drinking liquor and coffee are two of the capital sins of Mormonism. However, when they find out that the monks do neither, the Latter Day Saints may feel a slight glow of official sympathy.

On the whole, the prospects of the new Cistercian foundation are very bright. They have a difficult task to perform, but everything is in their favor: and above all, they have an admirably chosen site.

Thanks to the untiring efforts of the late Monsignor Wilfrid J. Giroux of Ogden they secured what one of their friends described as the "best ranch in Utah." Monsignor Patrick Kennedy who has taken Monsignor

Giroux's place in Ogden has also stepped into his role of the monks' best friend and has been joined by many others, both Catholic and non-Catholic, who have gone out of their way to surmise and cater to the Cistercians' every need.

One thing, however, must be clear. The work which the monks have come to do in Utah is above all the work of contemplation. What will no doubt have the most forcible immediate effect on their neighbors will be their "agricultural apostolate," their transformation of an arid valley into an Eden of orchards and gardens. But this is only secondary. The Cistercian vocation is the work that excels all other works and that is performed in silence, in the depths of the soul. They have an apostolate, it is true, but it is an apostolate not of action but of union with God. Their apostolate is to fill themselves from the source of living waters, that grace may flow, through them, into the whole Church, and any rival enterprise that clouds the purity of heart on which this vocation depends, tends necessarily to diminish the efficacy of the monks' work in the Church. Their main concern must therefore always be to empty themselves of solicitude for created things in order to be filled with the obscure light and the dark fire of the Divinity of the Word, drawing them into Himself and uniting them to the Father by the bond of the Holy Spirit. This purity of heart which constitutes the monk's gift of himself to the action of God's love is the most powerful of means for bringing grace down upon the world.

This second Cistercian foundation in three years will soon be followed by the first establishment of Trappistine nuns in the United States. The site has already been selected in the Archdiocese of Boston and forty-nine applications have already been received. All these facts come together to point to the final perfecting and maturing of the Church in America. Without a full representation of the contemplative Orders, we cannot yet say, with complete confidence, that we have come of age. There are still one or two gaps, and perhaps the time has come when these too will be filled. Not the least significant date in the history of American Catholicism would be the foundation of a first American Charterhouse. Will the Carthusians come to our mountains and forests soon? The land is full of grand solitudes that await the semi-eremitical Orders. Whether they come to fill up the measure of the perfect age of Christ in us depends largely on our own bishops. We hope it will be soon.

The Barren Tree

✶

GEORGE N. SHUSTER

GEORGE N. SHUSTER, *who served as managing editor of* The Commonweal *until 1939, is now president of Hunter College in New York. He is the author of* The Catholic Spirit in Modern English Literature, The Germans, *and other books.*

✶

AGAIN we have had Good Friday, and the unveiling of the Rood. This is the Tree, we said, on which the Saving of the world was grown. Tree of the knowledge of good and evil; tree of Jesse; tree of man's redeeming: these three, and what more is possibly to be said of good and evil? But there is also the barren tree. It is the theme of a haunting passage in Mr. Santayana's book, dealing with the Gospel episode in which the Savior angrily rebukes the fig tree for not bearing figs. This tree, as Santayana observes, was not at fault. It had not willfully made up its mind to be barren. Nevertheless the Savior found it accursed; and our author goes on to say: "It is not on voluntary naughtiness, not on conscious sins, that divine punishment falls most heavily and irremediably. For such sins there is possible repentance, and they are, after all, groping after a good, however ill-chosen. The final curse falls on constitutional blindness, on self-sufficiency, on obduracy in not recognizing divine opportunities."

These are terrible words. The light that is hidden under a bushel is snuffed out. A man who does not hear is deaf forever. When the city does not realize that her Lord is at the gate, a blight is on the streets. Can these things be true? The Christian faith replies with vehemence, and all the great religious philosophies answer assentingly. Not to have clapped one's ears tight when the small voice spoke is the secret spring of all holiness, whether it be that of Socrates or Francis. And so—one asks the question anxiously—may it not be that the desperate evil by which the modern time has suffered and by which it has now irrevocably died, was a curious, half unconscious self-sufficiency? An obduracy which strangely fancied that it was tenderness? Did not men assume that by willing themselves into an intellectual and moral dimension of their own devising they could build more splendid mansions for their egos? It was neither an unpleasant nor a knowingly immoral life they desired to live. In the new realm, music flowed on during the day and the night. The theme was always benevolence, improvement, tolerance, enlightenment. Excelsior! And when there was conversation, it had to do with the equality of human beings. The good things of life—raiment and drink with which the lily of the field is not concerned—were to be meted out to all equally, piece by piece, cup by cup.

And from this new world, so cannily planned, which could be unrestrainedly cruel because in its own way it wanted so much to be kind, God ominously departed, not for the reason that His presence was not desired but because He was relished only as an equal—a fellow citizen, a co-worker; perhaps a confrère. So that He should become only this and nothing more, notable poets and thinkers defined Him as an extension of humanity's own highest aspirations. Indeed, some said, was He not Himself being slowly born of man's experience during hours when he transcended (superseded) His humanity? Frequently it seemed inconvenient, even embarrassing, to admit that Christ had in fact existed. Efforts were therefore made to interpret the Testament as a Goethean, a Celtic, an Aryan fiction. Yet in the end these attempts seemed not in keeping with the canons of history, of which men were likely to be proud because by acquiescing in such rules they could lend to the study of themselves a soothing rigor, not unlike that which the ballplayer derives from the earnest pursuit of calisthenics. Therefore, it was almost everywhere conceded that the Savior had lived and had been an unusually good man. The Sermon on the Mount was, of course, mere poetry, but it was excellent fantasy and a credit to the human race. At the metamorphosis involved no one seemed to marvel greatly. For how could much importance attach to it in a time when the absence of miracles had led to the working of the greatest of all wonders, namely those of science? God had not merely become man in a new and quite blasphemous sense. He was slowly transformed into one of the aspects of Nature. And since man was gradually conquering nature, there could be little enough doubt that in the end the *anima vagula blandula* would hold Divinity in its hands ere it died.

Let us close our eyes and look back, away from the concentration camps and the piebald dictators of our time. Is it possible to avoid feeling that while men busy at their well-intentioned words scarce noticed, God faded out of human history? Or rather did He not steal gently away, as the radiance goes almost imperceptibly from the twilight sky? In quite the selfsame way the fig tree ceased to bear fruit. It still put forth leaves and limbs—limbs and leaves only. You sense that men, too, in the customary sense of the term, were innocent. Kant turned, and saw the Lord had not yet gone. He ran after the Master, but somehow there was no catching up any longer. Comte said that he would build new tabernacles, not because there was any dearth of those but because the deity to be enshrined would insist upon a liturgy quite his own, harmonious and well instructed.

Those of our fathers who did not move with the tide, who knelt in their parish fanes beside mission crosses and statues of the Sacred Heart, had neither literature nor philosophy nor art. The share allotted to them in the business of subduing the forces of physical creation was a very small one, indeed. Lord Acton for his part spoke of a tradition of social orderliness which had lain round the youth of Christendom, but the very thought of trying to revive it hardly seemed a practical intellectual enterprise. Others wrote in journals few bothered to read, and set down angry words about the life around them. Inevitably, however, that life coursed even in our fathers' veins. Pasteur measured his faith against that of a Breton peasant. Yet this peasant himself began to spend his Sundays leaning against the bar of a bistro. Generations might have despaired save that of their tribulation and loneliness sanctity was almost profligately born. Saint Therese rose like a star above Lisieux. And there appeared a miraculous galaxy of other stars.

Oddly enough, there was an undiscerned affinity between the asceticism of the saints and that of the scientist. No quarrel here. Until the hour of midnight chemist and bacteriologist, physicist and geologist, picked their way through the labyrinth of reality. They followed a rigid ritual in the shrine of truth. But somehow they did not know they did this. I have watched great scientists practice a poignant self-renouncement—have seen their faces resemble the countenances of penitential religious because of the luminous austerity that shone in them. But nobody knew this was so. Nor did more than a few realize how with each new discovery man was being driven away from every mooring save that of refuge in the harbor of things as they are.

And so the barren tree has withered. The leaves which have fallen and withered are the sons and daughters of men.

I shall not try to describe what they look like when they die. Let us have just a few words about how they died. There has been no blessing on their going. Today I can still remember how, as a boy, I first encountered death as an enterprise. The hour had come for my great-uncle to go, and all his kin were summoned from far and near so that he could impart to each one a blessing, and so that they might help him on his journey. It was clear that he was setting forth on great business, for which solemn preparation must be made; and though he found it hard to leave, and knew there would be no returning, he laid by the store of such goods and treasures as he might use in that undiscovered country to which his soul was repairing. And for three days after, we stood, as it were, on the pier from which he had sailed, waving our best wishes in the midst of our tears. My great-uncle was a humble though a learned man. But when he set forth he was given the same right of citizenship in the new state as was accorded to kings, and the Church opened unto him all her store.

Now I have read the manuscript of the most horrible book known to me. It is the story of the business of death as conducted by Concentration Camps, Inc. This is not a tale of individual outrages, but rather a carefully written account of killing when the principles of efficiency and the methods of science are intelligently employed. It was possible, at the end, to transform a motley thousand human beings from living, breathing bundles of nerves and blood vessels and bones to fertilizer within a few hours. Nor is that much more horrible than was the enterprise of slaughter as conducted by the masters of the science of bombing. This story has not yet been written. We used to shudder when some fascist commented on the beauty of bursting grenades on the Ethiopian plains. But that is awfully dated. At Warsaw, Dresden and Hiroshima, death really became a wholesale business. We can only hope that the children who perished in the Dresden meadow one awful night will not rise in the bodies which then lay there. For if so Heaven would be hell.

Indeed, is it too much to say that when God departed from human history, the gates of hell were opened? We may well ask that question in penitence and fear. Santayana writes at the close of his book: "The idea of Christ has had many worshippers and has inspired many saints. But it has not converted the world or saved it. The world does not wish to be saved. If we say that the world thereby wills its own damnation, we are merely venting our private displeasure, without frightening the world." These are once more terrible words. We may hope they are not true.

The world will not be converted by the shudder which now runs up and down its spine. That will in the end drive men only to sacrifice all else, even freedom, to self-preservation. I think we shall put shackles on ourselves so that our fingers may be kept away from the atomic bomb. Conversion, saving, will come only when, having sensed that his own miracles have only the ruthless automatism of nature in them, man will pray for the miracle of love which he has not the power to perform. It seems to me that the mind of man is beginning once more so to pray in a humility as unconscious as was its self-sufficiency. It prays with blood on its hands without quite knowing how that blood got there. It prays without knowing to whom it prays. And therewith, perhaps—we can only hope because hope is a virtue—the curse may be lifted again from the barren tree.